P9-DHL-559

CONTENTS

FOR GEORGE A. ROMERO,
CHEF DE CUISINE OF THE LIVING DEAD

11:59 AM

ZT&T

BITER

SEARCH

TOP STORIES

MYSTERIOUS OUTBREAK CAUSES RESTAURANT HAVOC

Be aware of the danger signs: bluish skin color, bulging eyes, inability to speak, and/or noisy breathing. DO NOT attempt the Heimlich maneuver on anyone exhibiting these symptoms. Instead, watch for signs of inappropriate table habits. If a patron attempts to bite a fellow diner or server, immediately pierce their skull with a sharp object such as a steak knife. Reports that the outbreak is foodborne remain unsubstantiated. However the local food scene is feeling the effects. The Happy Gastronome has discontinued its popular brunch due to complaints of body parts in the hash. Lulu's on Willow has closed after a party of five, having waited two hours for a table, devoured the hostess. Obligatory take-out is becoming standard as many restaurants can no longer

ONE
APPETIZERS
FOR AN APOCALYPSE

ANY WAY YOU SLICE IT

elveeta? What good was processed cheese against the living dead?

Pam choked back a sob so her kids, searching in the next aisle, wouldn't think she was losing it. She never would have allowed Velveeta into her house before. But right now she needed foods that never expired. Undead cheese was better than no cheese at all.

All that mattered now was how you lived and how you ate. The survivors who had tried to make it on Diet Pepsi and Funyuns had quickly been run down and bitten, had risen up again, and now fed mindlessly on the living. So in some ways, not a lot had changed.

She had to get what they needed and get them out of this supermarket. She didn't know what else might be here. She took some of the deathless cheese. Since the outbreak she had done her best to keep her family fed. But in a world ruled by the hungry dead, it was snack or be snacked on.

Food was her connection to people. When she was still just a scruffy redneck girl in the Georgia mountains, she'd tried to impress a shy boy named Daryl with cheese sandwiches. He'd shown her how to butcher a squirrel with a hatchet. "First you chop the head," he'd said, guiding her hand on the hatchet with his. She started making him lunch every day after that, just wanting to touch his hand again. Where there were snacks there was hope.

She froze. There was that sucking sound, like a stuck drain, or the last slurp of milkshake through a straw. The sound they made right before they bit you. She drew a butcher's cleaver from her purse and listened as the noise came again, closer this time.

"*Stahhhhp!*" came a boy's whine. "Mom, Ronnie's not cooperating!"

She stomped into the next aisle.

"God *damn* it, Veronica!" she said, gesturing. "You scare your little brother like that one more time, so help me I'm gonna leave you on the highway. And, Earl—"

She stopped herself. She was brandishing the cleaver at her own teenage daughter and eight-year-old son. She lowered the blade slowly.

The girl rolled her eyes at Pam and made the sucking sound again, sending the boy off howling.

"You help me find him," Pam hissed at the expressionless teen. "Anything happens to him, it's on you, you hear me?"

Veronica rolled her eyes again and sauntered indifferently in the direction Earl had fled.

How had her darling princess become such a monster? Pam wondered how she'd made it this far, wrangling two bored kids with rocketing hormones and plummeting blood sugar.

Damn it, where was Earl?

Rushing past the condiments she heard the slurping again. She drew a breath for another telling-off when she collided with a teenage boy in a crumpled paper hat, knocking him into a bin of moldy produce.

As she instinctively reared back, she corrected herself: a *former* teenage boy. His skin was dark gray, all the color bled from his eyes, and he was missing most of his left cheek. A stockboy's apron caked with dried entrails hung loose from his neck. He champed at her viciously with broken teeth loosely tinseled with wrecked braces.

Now she understood why no one had gotten the Velveeta.

Before the dead boy could find his balance, she swung her cleaver sidelong at the base of his skull, just as Daryl had taught her to butcher the squirrel. A crunch like celery, and his head lolled with a sickening gush of dark fluid. The fallen head continued to slurp and roll its eyes at her.

Damn thing's still a teen, she thought.

She raised the cleaver over her head with both hands, and split the surly face like a pumpkin.

Sorry, kid. This had once been a boy Ronnie's age, with parents, friends, and involuntary boners. Now he was cleanup in aisle 6, and no one to mop it up. That was just the hand they'd been dealt.

The apocalypse ain't no picnic.

A BRUNCH IN THE GUT

The morning before the world ended, Pam Beaumont found herself with her back pressed hard against someone else's kitchen door, heart racing like a squirrel's. A dozen ravenous guests had already infested the living room. *A freaking swarm,* she thought. *And they're early.*

She could hear them through the door. All she had to fend them off was a platter of stuffed mushrooms.

Brunch always meant trouble, but she had only agreed to cater her friend Stacy's birthday because Pam loved to cook. She had discovered her passion one summer making sandwiches for Daryl, the biggest crush she'd ever had: food could bring you closer to people you couldn't even talk to. It was her connection to humanity.

The birthday guests were drawn to the irresistible smell of bacon. All except for Penny Morton, who looked pale, gray even, and stumbled oddly around the gift table. *Drunk at this hour. Good lord.* Pam set the platter down on the coffee table and retreated to the kitchen.

When she returned, she found Penny bent double over Stacy, who lay still on the floor, her birthday crown rolling toward the door.

Penny had her mouth clamped awkwardly on Stacy's lower face. *If that's CPR, she's doing it wrong,* thought Pam, and she moved instinctively to push the woman aside.

Penny's shoulder was hot as an oven—and she was yanking tendons like wires from Stacy's throat with her teeth.

Brunches were just cursed.

Everyone had fled the room, except a guest who was about to bring the platter of mushrooms down on the gray ghoul's head. He missed and the platter flew to pieces around Pam's skull.

A deafening wind filled her head. She had just enough time to marvel at how wonderfully pink the birthday girl's windpipe was, before the world flickered and blew out like a pilot light.

GUTTED MUSHROOMS WITH BACON AND SPINACH

makes 20 stuffed mushrooms

6 strips bacon

½ red onion, diced

2 garlic cloves, finely chopped

20 large button mushrooms, stems removed

1 (10-ounce) package frozen chopped spinach, thawed

½ cup cream cheese, softened

Salt and freshly ground black pepper to taste

½ cup grated Parmesan cheese

1 Preheat the oven to 400°F.

2 In a large skillet, cook the bacon until browned and crisp. Transfer to a paper towel–lined plate to cool. Spoon off all but 1 tablespoon bacon fat from the pan. Add the onion and sauté until tender, about 5 minutes. Stir in the garlic and remove from the heat to cool completely.

3 Wipe the mushroom caps clean. Crumble the bacon. Put the spinach in a sieve, set it over the sink, and using your hands and a death grip, squeeze out as much liquid as you can.

4 In a large bowl, smash together the spinach, bacon, cream cheese, red onion mixture, salt, and pepper. Fill the mushroom caps with the mixture and set them on a baking sheet. Sprinkle the Parmesan on top.

5 Bake until the cheese is golden brown, about 15 minutes. Serve warm.

 PRO TIP

Walkers are attracted by sounds, bright light, and the smell of people, but they can't smell bacon. Quickly sort biters from survivors with the powerful aroma of bacon.

THE
DEAD 'ZONE

Pam woke in semi-darkness. Next to her, Penny Morton lay still and cold, her crushed head surrounded by plate shards and stale mushrooms. On the other side of her Pam could make out Stacy. Her friend's belly had been torn open and oozed a thick, clotted pulp. She looked like a half-eaten calzone.

Pam screamed and burst out of the house into the night, running dazed down the street. She had to get home to her kids.

As she rounded the corner, a man in a seersucker suit slowly turned to glare at her with furious pale eyes. He made a stuck drain sound.

Then he tried to bite her. "Asshole!" she yelled.

Someone dashed out of a dark storefront across the street right as the gory molester fumbled for her. A metallic flash traced a wide arc in the moonlight, and the man's head flew open with a wet slosh. A tall guy with a tattoo, stubble, and some kind of spade-like weapon helped her up.

"Get up, lady, them walkers are everywhere," he commanded. She followed in spite of herself. He was bossy and gruff like her ex-husband.

Inside the storefront was a pizza joint. The windows had been covered with tablecloths and the only light came from candles on the counter.

"Did you just kill that man with a pizza shovel?" she asked.

He peered outside through a small hole in the tablecloth. "It's a pizza *peel*," he corrected. "And that guy was already dead. Biters, walkers, whatever you call them. You got to mash their brains."

The image of half-eaten Stacy, oozing juicily, came to her unbidden. "Oh my God," she sobbed.

"Don't you know what's been going on?" he said as he wiped the blood from the pizza peel with a sponge.

She shook her head.

"Well, I'll tell you what I've seen, what they're saying on the radio, but I can't explain jack. I mean, power on and off, dead people waking up and going cannibal, government falling apart . . ."

He thrust the peel into the large gas oven and pulled out a knot of dough. He held it out to her.

"Anyhoo, we're still cooking with gas here. Name's Trey. Calzone?"

OOZING THREE-CHEESE CALZONE

serves 2

Extra-virgin olive oil, as needed

¾ cup fresh ricotta

1 ounce Parmesan cheese, grated (¼ cup)

2 tablespoons chopped basil

¼ teaspoon freshly ground black pepper

1 (8-ounce) ball pizza dough

⅓ cup tomato sauce

2 ounces fresh mozzarella, grated (½ cup)

1 Preheat the oven to 500°F. Line a rimmed baking sheet with foil and lightly oil.

2 In a bowl, stir together ricotta, Parmesan, basil, and pepper.

3 Lightly flour the dough and pull or roll it to a 12-inch round. Spread ricotta mixture on half the dough, leaving a half-inch border all around. Brush edges of dough with water and fold dough over filling; pinch to seal.

4 Transfer the calzone to the prepared baking sheet. Brush the top of the dough with olive oil. Spoon tomato sauce over the calzone and sprinkle with mozzarella.

5 Transfer pan to the oven and bake until crust is firm and cheese is golden, about 15 minutes. Let cool 5 minutes before serving.

A long-handled metal pizza peel is an ideal weapon against the living dead. The aluminum blade can be sharpened on three sides. A strong forward thrust will decapitate at a safe distance from the wielder. Be sure to rinse well with bleach before using again with pizza.

THE
CHIPS ARE DOWN

She rushed headlong through her empty house.

"Earl, honey? Ronnie!" Her gut churned at the silence. All she heard was a distant scraping.

Best-case scenario, Earl's babysitter had taken them someplace safe. "Lindsay, you here?"

Worst-case . . .

Earl's SpongeBob backpack wasn't in its usual place. Ronnie's phone charger was gone, too. On the table was a half-eaten plate of the kale chips Lindsay made for the kids most afternoons. *Kale chips!* There was hope.

A chair had been knocked against the pantry, and there was a pink Post-it on the door. She moved the chair to get a better look at the note: an O above an X in red crayon. Maybe a hurried good-bye note?

Something brushed the other side of the door.

Out from the pantry stumbled Lindsay, her outsized white teeth bared in rabid fury, her pretty blue eyes blanched to yellow. She shambled hungrily toward Pam.

An O above an X. Skull and crossbones. Ronnie's sense of humor. Good lord.

Pam pulled a handle from her knife block, and threatened her kids' babysitter with a meat cleaver. She gripped it like a hatchet.

Lindsay gnashed her teeth at Pam. Pam remembered half-eaten Stacy and covered her neck with one hand, gripping her cleaver in the other. Lindsay gurgled and lunged for Pam's belly.

"That's enough!" Pam aimed. *You got to mash their brains.*

Pam had excellent knife skills. Lindsay staggered back, spilling kale chips across the floor. The scattered chips crunched as she collapsed on top of them.

Pam fell to her knees, unable to breathe. Rage and frustration burned in her throat. She still had to find her kids. And where the hell was she going to find another sitter who could cook like that?

DESICCATED CRISPY KALE CHIPS
serves 6 to 8

**1 large bunch of kale, torn into bite-size pieces,
washed and thoroughly dried**

¼ cup extra-virgin olive oil

¾ teaspoon kosher salt

Chili powder, for sprinkling

1 Preheat the oven to 350°F.

2 Make sure the kale is very dry; if not, it won't get crisp in the oven.
In a large bowl, toss kale pieces with olive oil and kosher salt—you
may need to do this in 2 batches—to combine well. Massage the oil
onto each kale piece until the oil is evenly distributed and the kale
is shiny. Spread the kale out on two jelly roll pans (you will need
to do this in 2 batches). Bake the kale chips for 12 to 16 minutes,
checking on it after 12. If the leaves look crispy and crumble, the
chips are ready—otherwise, bake for another 2 minutes and check
again. Remove from the oven and allow to cool to room temperature.

3 Toss the kale with the salt and the chili powder to taste.

 Carry snacks that won't turn. Kale chips keep, and they
will have you in fighting form for a long time.

I SCREAM,
YOU SCREAM

The car was missing, and the spare key was gone from its hiding place. The thought of Ronnie driving Earl away was both a huge relief and terrifying. Ronnie wasn't old enough to drive, no matter what her ex-husband thought.

She knew they'd be hungry. She filled a duffel bag with kitchen tools and food that would keep, tucked the cleaver in her belt, then watched and waited. Once the biter herd in the street thinned, she crept with her cargo from the door to her neighbor's driveway.

She tried her neighbor's blue minivan. The car alarm made her jump and she dropped the bag. The biters swerved to follow the noise. She'd have to come back for it.

A biter in running shorts stood slurping between her and a truck across the street. As she made for the truck the walker struggled to keep up. He shambled far too slowly to stay with her.

As a girl Pam had run free all over the mountains near her home. That's how she met Daryl, out shooting squirrel for his dinner. He had been going to eat the thing raw. She had thought with a little effort she could make it better. She'd asked him to show her how to butcher the critter. He'd put her hand at the bottom of the hatchet handle so she could get leverage. She had found she liked butchering it.

It wasn't that different with the cleaver. The biter in running gear slowly hobbled toward her.

She held the cleaver like a hatchet, waited until he got close, then calmly plunged it into his frontal lobe. Runners annoyed her.

She managed to open the truck door, twisted the key in the ignition, and yelped as an insipid jingle blared from a loudspeaker on top of the truck.

Attracted by the ear-piercing racket, biters stumbled out from all around and began clawing and thumping at the sides of the vehicle.

She had commandeered an ice cream truck.

COLD-BLOODED ICE CREAM BREAD SANDWICHES

serves 8

1 pint premium ice cream, in any flavor you like, softened

1½ cups self-rising flour (or use 1½ cups all-purpose flour mixed with 2 teaspoons baking powder and ½ teaspoon salt)

1 pint premium ice cream, in any flavor complementary to your first flavor (vanilla goes with everything), slightly softened

1 Preheat the oven to 350°F. Grease an 8- or 9-inch loaf pan and line with parchment paper. Grease the parchment paper.

2 In a large bowl, whisk the softened ice cream until smooth. Stir in the flour until just combined. Pour the mixture into the prepared loaf pan and bake for 40 to 45 minutes, or until an inserted toothpick comes out clean. Let pan cool on a wire rack for 10 to 15 minutes, unmold the loaf from the pan, and then let cool completely on the rack.

3 Slice the bread into ½-inch pieces and make sandwiches with the remaining ice cream. Freeze for at least 20 minutes before serving.

 When the power grid is down, mobile engine-powered refrigeration will keep vital food fresh—for as long as you can find diesel to siphon.

TELL IT TO
THE COWS

Meat is murder, you know."

Trey looked up from his plate of FEMA mystery meat at the girl in a black hoodie with a skull silkscreened on the front.

"Tell that to the douchebags who ate my delivery guy," he said, pushing his plate back on the school cafeteria table.

The girl scooped a chip into a Tupperware tub of guacamole. She frowned and passed the chip to a boy sitting next to her. She had her arm draped awkwardly around his shoulders.

"You didn't get that stuff here," he said.

"Obviously," she said. "It's totally vegan. Made it before we came. Is that your shovel?"

"It's called a pizza peel."

"Do you bake, or fight with your shovel?"

"Both. Works quiet, never runs out of ammo."

"You killed some, didn't you."

"They were already dead."

The girl reflected for a moment. "I locked my babysitter in a closet."

He raised an eyebrow.

"She caught a fever and woke up all angry and flesh-eating. My brother lured her into the pantry with my gerbil Ossie as bait."

She glared at the boy, but kept him in her protective embrace.

"I'm making for Fort Benning," he said. "Army's there, it should be safe."

"That's OK. I'm driving us to my dad's place in Griffin in my mother's car. She's missing."

Trey nodded gravely. *Jesus, this child ain't old enough to drive.*

"OK, then," he said. "How about a caravan? Guess Griffin's on my way. Safety in numbers and whatnot."

She looked him in the face for the first time. "You going to protect us with your *peel*?" She handed him a chip.

"I don't guess you need much saving," he said as he stood up.

"Truth is," she almost whispered, "I never felt so alive."

GUAC AND LOAD GUACAMOLE

serves 6

4 ripe avocado, halved and pitted
¾ teaspoon salt, or more to taste
Juice of ½ lime, or more to taste
2 tablespoons chopped fresh cilantro
1 scallion, white and green parts, minced
1 jalapeno pepper, seeds and veins removed, minced
Few drops hot sauce, optional
Corn chips, for serving

Using a spoon, scoop the avocado flesh into a bowl. Add the remaining ingredients and smash forcefully with a fork, leaving the mixture a little chunky. Taste and correct seasonings, adding more salt and/or lime juice as needed. Serve with chips.

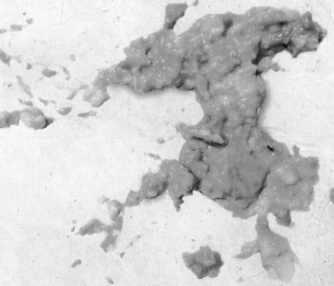

 A vegetable-based diet is likely to become more attractive when you think about why the living dead find you so delicious.

WHEN YOU LEAST
EXPECT THEM

You had to admit, she'd been killing it these past few days.

She'd, what, like saved her annoying little brother from a cannibal babysitter, driven her mom's car like a NASCAR superstar, and whipped up a batch of vegan hummus from crappy cafeteria supplies. Now she stood shoulder to shoulder with the dozen or so survivors who hadn't turned or fled, against an advancing pack of the living dead. And there was no one there to say she couldn't. *LOL*

She considered what might be the humane way to kill a walker. She had swiped a long bread knife from the school kitchen. The slurping mob of biters was pushing hard against the perimeter fence around the FEMA center. Trey raised his pizza shovel. The fence bowed inward. *I so got this.*

"When's Mom coming?" her brother asked. She had stopped even answering days ago. She squeezed his shoulder and tried to smile. He gave her the side-eye, then ran inside the school.

A section of the fence gave way and toppled like an avalanche of sleighbells. At the same moment there came a racket of demented chimes from down the block. The walkers swerved toward the loud noise. *WTF?*

Trey raised an eyebrow as an ice cream truck rounded the corner, loudspeaker blaring. Out from the ridiculous truck jumped a woman in a blood-covered apron, and she started splitting walker heads like canned chickpeas with a hatchet. Or wait—was it a cleaver?

When the woman had cut down all fifteen walkers, she waved to the refugees. "Veronica?" she called.

The girl pulled her hood down over her face. *OMG OMG OMFG. My mother just climbed out of an ice cream truck covered in brains.*

"Ronnie! Thank goodness, I've been searching for you for two days. Where's Earl?"

"Mother," she said barely controlling her exasperation, "it's Nica now. Not 'Ronnie.'"

Please kill me now.

POSTHUMOUS RED CHILE HUMMUS

makes 2 cups

2 garlic cloves

¼ teaspoon crushed red chile flakes

1 tablespoon plus ⅓ cup olive oil

2 (15.5-ounce) cans chickpeas, drained,
⅓ cup liquid reserved

3 tablespoons freshly squeezed lemon juice

1 tablespoon tahini

½ teaspoon salt, or more to taste

Freshly ground black pepper to taste

Pinch ground cumin

Pita chips, for serving, optional

Raw veggies, for serving, optional

1 Violently smash the garlic with the side of a knife, then pull off the peels. Finely chop one garlic clove and leave the other whole. Heat a small skillet over medium heat, then add the chile flakes and let toast for 15 seconds. Add 1 tablespoon of the oil and the whole smashed garlic clove and sauté until the garlic is softened and lightly browned, 2 to 3 minutes. Remove from heat.

2 In a food processor, combine the chickpeas, remaining olive oil, lemon juice, tahini, salt, chopped garlic, sautéed garlic (but not the red chile oil), and pepper to taste. Blend until smooth, adding the reserved chickpea liquid as needed, until it reaches the desired consistency.

3 Spread the hummus on a large plate and drizzle with the chile oil. Sprinkle evenly with the cumin. Serve with pita chips or raw veggies, if desired.

 PRO TIP   Most people will leave canned chickpeas behind, so look in the back of abandoned cupboards.

HOW IT
CRUMBLES

How are we ever gonna get past them?" asked Trey. "They'll smell us right off."

The duffel bag containing Pam's vital ingredients and cooking tools was right where she had dropped it. But it was surrounded by a milling throng of her deceased former neighbors.

They'd had to leave the FEMA center. The food was all gone, except for a wedge of overripe Camembert. Coffee-deprived refugees started to resemble walkers themselves, and the one or two who wandered out to look for a Starbucks never returned.

So they packed up Trey's pizza delivery van and the ice cream truck, after disabling its loudspeaker, and returned to Pam's house to try to rescue the only things that might keep them from having to live on dry cereal.

"Ronnie, bring me the cheese," said Pam.

"Mother, it's Nica. And I'm not going near that stinky product of animal oppression."

Pam got the Camembert herself, and she and Trey smeared themselves in the smelly ooze.

"Good lord, what a stink," Trey said.

Gagging all the way, they crept past the confused walkers, who looked at them a little suspiciously. When they got to the duffel they found two guys in aprons, draped in rotten fish, kneeling over the gear. The two reeking pairs stared at each other.

"That's my stuff," Pam whispered grimly.

"Finders keepers," said the first guy. "Man, you stink a lot worse than us."

Neither side would let go of the duffel bag handle. Finally Pam broke the stalemate.

"I'll make you a deal," she said. "You give me the bag, I'll make you some cookies. Real good ones."

The men considered her offer.

"Deal," one finally said. "But you better shower first, lady."

VIRULENTLY INFECTIOUS BUTTERSCOTCH CHOCOLATE CHIPPERS

makes 2 dozen cookies

2¼ cups all-purpose flour

1 teaspoon baking soda

1 teaspoon salt

1 cup (2 sticks) unsalted butter, softened

1½ cups packed dark brown sugar

2 tablespoons vanilla extract

2 large eggs

1 cup semisweet chocolate chips

1 cup butterscotch chips

Flaky sea salt

1   Preheat the oven to 375°F and line a large rimmed baking sheet with parchment paper.

2   In a medium bowl, combine the flour, baking soda, and salt.

3   In a large bowl with a hand mixer or in the bowl of a stand mixer, forcefully beat butter, brown sugar, and vanilla extract until creamy and subdued. Add eggs, one at a time, beating well after each addition. Gradually beat in the flour mixture. Using a spatula, fold in the chocolate and butterscotch chips. Drop dough by rounded tablespoons onto the baking sheet and sprinkle with flaky sea salt. Bake for 12 to 15 minutes, or until cookies are nicely browned and crisp. Transfer to a wire rack to cool before serving.

 PRO TIP

Bring hostile survivor groups together with baskets of cookies and other treats. Baked goods are the foundation upon which future civilization will be rebuilt.

I'LL STOP THE WORLD
AND MELT

Quick stab like *that*, you take his head right off," said Trey. He gave a mock thrust of his pizza peel at a gurgling dead state trooper. "Meanwhile the pole keeps 'em a few feet away."

First you chop the head . . . Her first love had taught her that many years ago. She wondered where Daryl was now. Still tracking squirrels in the Blue Ridge Mountains?

Even now she could see his sleepy sexy eyes, his sleeveless shirt, the way he'd only steal quick glances at her. Once when he'd skinned a squirrel with his hatchet, he had seemed almost embarrassed for the exposed little creature. Then he ate its liver.

She could never quite tell how he felt about her, but she had known they'd had some kind of connection. He'd told her he'd always protect her from monsters. Even a chupacabra. She had believed him.

"Once we cut this squirrel up," she had said, "how about we melt some cheese on it?"

She came out of her reverie as the undead state trooper tried to move forward between two abandoned cars on the highway. Trey just bumped him back again with the peel.

Pam was impressed, the weapon was even better than her cleaver. Trey put the peel in her hands from behind.

"Like this," he said softly as they beheaded the man together. The state trooper's head fell from his shoulders with a splat. She felt herself melting a little.

Why do I always fall for the bad boys?

"Now we're done with this asshole," she said, drawing her cleaver, "who wants quesadillas?"

DIESEL-STRENGTH QUESADILLAS
makes 3 split-level quesadillas (serves 6 to 8 as an appetizer)

LIME PICKLED JALAPEÑOS
Juice of 2 limes (about ¼ cup)
½ teaspoon granulated sugar
Pinch coarse kosher salt
1 jalapeño, seeded if desired and thinly sliced

QUESADILLAS
4 tablespoons olive oil
1 small yellow onion, thinly sliced
1 red bell pepper, thinly sliced
Coarse salt
Freshly ground black pepper
½ pound spicy pork sausage, casings removed

½ teaspoon paprika
¼ teaspoon cayenne pepper
2 tablespoons finely chopped cilantro, divided
12 six-inch corn or flour tortillas
2 cups shredded Monterey Jack cheese (about ½ pound)
½ cup sour cream, for serving

1 Prepare the jalapeños: In a bowl combine lime juice, sugar, and salt. Stir in the jalapeños. Let sit at room temperature for at least 1 hour.

2 Make the quesadillas: In a large skillet over medium-high heat add 1 tablespoon oil. Add the onion and bell pepper and season with salt and pepper. Sauté until the onions and peppers are tender, 7 to 12 minutes, then transfer to a plate.

3 Add 1 tablespoon of the oil to the pan and place back over medium-high heat. Add the sausage, paprika, and cayenne, and cook, stirring frequently, until the pork is cooked through, 5 to 7 minutes. Stir in 1 tablespoon of the cilantro.

4 Preheat the broiler. Place the tortillas in a single layer on two baking sheets and brush with remaining oil. Broil until toasted, about 2 minutes.

5 Divide the sausage among 3 tortillas and sprinkle each with 2 tablespoons cheese. Sprinkle ¼ cup cheese over another 3 of the tortillas. Top 3 more tortillas each with 2 tablespoons cheese and a third of the pepper-onion mixture. Leave the last 3 tortillas plain. Broil tortillas in batches until the cheese melts, 2 to 3 minutes.

6 Transfer a sausage-topped tortilla to a plate and sprinkle with the remaining cilantro. Top with a cheese tortilla, then a vegetable tortilla, then a plain tortilla. Cut into 4 wedges. Repeat and serve with the pickled jalapeños and sour cream.

PRO TIP

The more time passes after the outbreak, the more ingredient substitutions will be necessary. The past is gone—learn to love what you can find now.

HEADLESS BODY
IN TOPLESS BAR

The biters had helped Trey kick his coffee habit, but they kind of dropped the ball on the booze thing.

"Let's just have a look," Trey called from the pizza van, pulling over at a roadside bar.

"'Billy's Topless'?" Pam read with a snort. "No thanks, I'll wait out here." She got out of the ice cream truck and practiced with the pizza peel.

The room was murky and stank of stale ick. A neat row of shot glasses, cloudy from evaporated shots, was lined up on the bar. Trey held Pam's cleaver out ahead of him as he and the kids looked around.

"Aw shit," Trey sighed.

"Ewwww!" said Ronnie, backing quickly across the room.

Slumped against the kegs behind the bar was a corpse darker than a spoiled banana, its headless neck a withered stump.

"Double-ewwww," said Ronnie again, nearly tripping over something.

At the foot of a little stage sat the bartender's head, skin drawn taut and leathery across its angry face. It was snapping its teeth and rolling its eyes. A bottle of Jack Daniels rested a few inches from its nose.

Trey winced. He knew how it felt.

He grabbed the whisky and doused the twitching head. Taking a pull from the bottle, he tossed a match on the head and watched it burn. The flaming alcohol smelled kind of good.

"Sure could use a bite to go with my drink," he called so Pam would hear.

Pam stabbed at the air with the peel and didn't respond.

VERY-LAST-CALL BAR NUTS

makes 2 cups

2 cups raw mixed nuts (such as cashews, pecans, and almonds)
3 tablespoons sesame seeds
1 tablespoon unsalted butter
3 tablespoons honey
2 tablespoons light brown sugar
½ teaspoon ground cinnamon
½ teaspoon coarse kosher salt
¼ teaspoon cayenne pepper
¼ teaspoon paprika

1 Preheat oven to 300°F. Line a baking sheet with a nonstick mat or parchment paper. Place the nuts in a single layer on the baking sheet and roast, stirring halfway through, until golden brown, about 10 minutes. On a separate baking sheet, spread out the sesame seeds and toast until lightly golden and fragrant, about 8 minutes.

2 In a small saucepan set over medium heat, combine the butter, honey, brown sugar, cinnamon, salt, cayenne, and paprika. Heat, stirring until the butter melts and the sugar and salt dissolve.

3 Remove the toasted nuts from the oven and transfer to a large mixing bowl. Pour the honey mixture over the nuts and quickly stir to coat. Add the sesame seeds, stir to incorporate, and return the mixture to the baking sheet in a single layer. Bake for 15 minutes, stirring frequently, until the nuts are golden and fragrant but not dark brown. Remove the pan from the oven and set aside to cool completely. Break up the mixture to serve.

Keep some salty proteins around for when you need to drown your sorrows to help absorb the alcohol. The last thing you need in an apocalypse is a hangover.

FRIENDLY FIRE

Come on out. It's not like we're gonna eat you!" laughed the hairy man with the big shotgun. He frowned. "But we'll be taking the food."

A half-dozen thugs had surrounded the ice cream truck. They had hunting rifles, crowbars, and tire irons. Ronnie and Earl had gone off for firewood before they arrived, and Pam was worried they would return at the wrong moment.

"We can't just give up," said Trey, hunkered on the truck floor. "This is all the food we've got."

Pam bristled. "What the hell are we gonna do about my kids? If anything happens to them, it's on me."

Through the window, Pam spotted movement on the horizon. She grabbed the hot plate, a pan, and some oil. "Get me the microphone for the loudspeaker and switch it on."

The bandit sang, "Little pig, little pig, let me in." He approached the back doors of the truck with a crowbar.

"Cover your ears," Pam told Trey.

BANG.

The booming pop made the bandit drop his crowbar. Then another bang, and a whole volley of reports like a machine gun.

The bandits threw themselves to the ground.

After a few seconds the leader smiled.

"That ain't no M-16, my friends. That sounds like popcorn."

The men laughed grimly and stood up again.

But the amplified popcorn had drawn a horde of gluttonous walkers. They lurched over en masse, and attacked the bandits until there wasn't a single one left uneaten.

When the walkers had wandered off again, Ronnie crawled out of the bushes where she'd been hiding and Trey resumed work on the engine. They'd have to hurry. Those walkers would be hungry again in an hour.

Pam looked around. *Where's Earl?*

SEMIAUTOMATIC GARLIC-PARMESAN POPCORN

serves 8

½ cup (1 stick) unsalted butter

2 garlic cloves, minced

½ teaspoon sweet paprika

½ teaspoon salt, plus more to taste

3 tablespoons olive oil

1 cup popcorn kernels

¾ cup grated Parmesan cheese

1 In a small saucepot over medium heat, melt the butter with the garlic, paprika, and salt. Cook for 1 minute, until the garlic is fragrant. Remove from the heat.

2 In a stock or pasta pot with a tight-fitting cover, over medium-high heat, add the olive oil and let heat for 30 seconds. Add the popcorn. When you begin to hear the kernels popping, shake the pan. Continue shaking the pan frequently to avoid burning. When the popping slows, remove from the heat and transfer to a large bowl. Drizzle with the garlic butter and Parmesan cheese. Toss to combine, adjust seasoning as needed, and enjoy.

Popcorn is rich in polyphenols, but be sure any walkers are out of earshot before enjoying.

PRETTY MUCH
FED ALREADY

Ronnie had gone out alone to search for her little brother. She was sick of being bossed by her mother, so she'd sneaked off. But now she was getting hungry.

She spotted Earl's SpongeBob backpack in a ditch by the road. In it she found half of an energy bar her mother had made to keep him quiet. How far could a second-grader go on half an energy bar?

As the sun sank lower, Ronnie grew tired. There was a playground off to the right and she sat down on a swing to eat what was left of the energy bar.

A faint shuffling sound came from a playhouse next to the sandbox. She stood up.

"Earl?" she called.

From the house emerged a tiny shape, a child much smaller than Earl, trailing a doll.

No, it wasn't a doll. It was somebody else's arm.

The toddler walker kept falling over and couldn't make much progress toward Ronnie.

Then a second child came out of the house. Another walker, larger, missing an arm.

It was her little brother. And as usual he was trying to bite her.

Ronnie drew a breath. She wanted to cry. *Oh, you little pest. My stupid little pest.*

She pulled the long string from her hood and ran toward Earl. She tried to tempt him with the energy bar.

"Come on, Earl. I brought you some food."

He was clutching something. When she got close she could see he had two long, fuzzy ears in his remaining hand, and his chin dripped with blood.

He was eating a bunny.

"Ewww! Earl, how could you? You are so disgusting."

TILL-YOU-DROP CHOCOLATE-CHERRY ENERGY BARS

makes 16 squares

2 cups walnuts, pecans, or cashews
⅓ cup unsweetened cocoa powder
¼ teaspoon salt
1½ cups pitted dates
1 cup dried cherries
1 cup granola

1 Place the nuts in a food processor and blend on high until they are finely ground.

2 Add the cocoa powder and salt. Pulse to combine.

3 Add the dates one at a time through the feed tube of the food processor while it is running. Add the dried cherries while the processor is running.

4 Press the mixture into an 8-by-8-inch pan and sprinkle with granola, pressing and pushing it into the cocoa mixture so it adheres. Place in the freezer or fridge for at least an hour or until firm. Cut into 16 squares and store in an airtight container in the fridge.

 Pack healthy goodies. A treat can keep children well behaved while you're busy saving them from reanimated corpses.

WINGS OF
DISASTER

Pam tossed a live chicken to Earl. The boy arched up and caught the cloud of feathers with his teeth. His mouth closed on the hen's breast, gave it a violent shake, and came away dripping red.

She wasn't surprised that he had turned. Earl had always been the first to catch whatever was going around the playground.

None of them could bear to end his existence, even as a walker, so they caught small animals to keep him calm. They were all exhausted from climbing trees to shake recently feral chickens from their roosts.

She watched him eat the still-moving bird and sighed. "I wish you could have the childhood I had," she said. "I wish you could play hide-and-seek, make mud pies, run free in the woods . . ."

As a girl she had felt free in the woods—away from awkwardness and people, away from their demands.

One day she had wandered deeper than usual into the woods near her house, when she saw a boy in a sleeveless shirt aiming a gun at a tree. He fired and a squirrel fell out of the tree.

He laid the squirrel gently on a log, then took a hatchet and chopped off its head. He started to open it up to skin it. He yanked out a couple of bits and ate them. She couldn't stop watching.

A twig snapped under her foot, and he caught her. Hiding his meal behind his back, he yelled at her to get the hell out of there.

She had no idea why, but she'd asked him to give it to her. She'd cooked it up for him. That was her way of making friends.

A helicopter roared overhead, making them jump. It appeared to release a cloud of fire on the town just over the ridge.

Had it come to this? Napalm, like some kind of pest control? Pam decided they had to get away from "civilization" as fast as possible.

Once Earl had gobbled his fill, they tied him up again and bundled him inside the truck with a sack over his head.

Trey eyed the chicken's wings, still twitching on the carcass.

"You know," he said to Pam, "we probably won't want to waste those."

NAPALM SPICY CHICKEN WINGS

serves 6 to 8

3 pounds chicken wings, patted dry with paper towels
Coarse kosher salt
Freshly ground black pepper
2 tablespoons peanut or vegetable oil, plus more to fry
6 tablespoons unsalted butter, melted
2 to 3 tablespoons honey
¼ cup Sriracha or hot sauce
2 limes, zested and juiced, plus lime wedges
for serving

1 Place the chicken wings in a large bowl and season generously with salt and pepper. Refrigerate, uncovered, for at least 30 minutes and up to 24 hours.

2 Preheat the oven to 400°F. Spread the chicken wings on a rimmed baking sheet in a single layer and drizzle with 2 tablespoons of the oil. Place in the oven and roast until the chicken wings are firm but not fully cooked through, about 20 minutes.

3 In a small saucepan over medium heat, melt the butter. Whisk in honey, Sriracha, and lime zest and simmer for 1 minute. Stir in lime juice and remove from the heat. Season with salt and pepper.

4 Using a large pot, pour in enough of the vegetable oil to reach 5 inches up the sides. Place over high heat and heat the oil until it registers 375°F (190°C) on a deep-fry thermometer.

5 Working in small batches, fry the wings, turning occasionally, until they are crisp and golden brown, 5 to 7 minutes. Use a slotted spoon to remove the wings from the oil and drain on a paper towel–lined baking sheet. Put the wings in a large bowl and toss with the Sriracha butter. Transfer to a platter and serve hot with additional lime wedges.

PRO TIP

Serve with
colorful cock-
tail napkins.
Unexpected
combat with
greasy hands
can cost lives.

HOW IS THAT
PREPARED?

Ronnie grabbed a key from her father's house and walked to the backyard, past two decaying pit bulls still chained to a post.

"Here," she said, testing the ground with her feet.

Trey peeled up a swatch of Astroturf and uncovered a damp metal door sunk in the lawn. Ronnie turned the key and pulled up hard.

"It's jammed," she said.

They had to attach the dogs' choke chains to the handle and pull them with the delivery van to loosen the stuck hatch. The door finally pulled open with a dry squeal. Sour air escaped from the hole.

Pam shook her head and started down the aluminum ladder holding a flashlight. She called her ex-husband's name.

"Ed, you down here? We need a place to stay. I got Ronnie with me. And Earl." She looked back at the truck. "Sort of."

A pathetic slurping sound answered from the dark hole. Pam shot back up the ladder.

Out of the hatch behind her popped a pale, chewed-up carcass in fatigues and the camo hunting hat she'd once bought her ex-husband for his birthday. His face was twisted with fury.

She hesitated, then dropped the hatch lid on him, cutting him in two. His top half crawled across the lawn and grabbed at her ankles until she brained him with the cleaver. Her ex oozed onto the neglected lawn.

The bunker was lined with a couple of iron bunks, a wide-screen TV, and metal shelves crammed with bottled water and canned food. One of the bunks held the corpse of Ed's younger second wife, Angela, her middle gnawed out.

"Guess they pretty much ate each other up," Trey remarked. "Ain't one of these cans been opened."

Pam sighed and slumped down on the lawn.

Just like you, Ed. Got yourself stuck in your own shelter with a ton of food and no can opener.

CRABBY PREPPER PUFFS

makes 16 crabby puffs (serves 6 to 8 as an appetizer)

8 ounces jumbo lump crabmeat, picked

1 shallot, finely chopped

2 lemons, zested and juiced

1 tablespoon mayonnaise

½ teaspoon Worcestershire

1 teaspoon hot sauce or Sriracha

2 scallions, thinly sliced (about 3 tablespoons)

Coarse kosher salt

Freshly ground black pepper

16 slices white bread

4 tablespoons unsalted butter, melted

1 In a medium bowl, mix together the crabmeat, shallot, lemon zest, half of the lemon juice, mayonnaise, Worcestershire, and hot sauce. Stir in three-quarters of the scallions and season with salt and pepper.

2 Use a 3-inch round cutter to cut the bread slices into rounds, and place the rounds on a baking sheet. (Save the scraps for bread crumbs if you like.)

3 Preheat the broiler. Whisk together the butter and the remaining lemon juice. Use a pastry brush to brush one side of each bread round with the lemon butter. Place under the broiler and broil until the rounds are golden brown, 30 to 45 seconds. Carefully flip over the rounds and brush with the remaining lemon butter. Top each with a heaping tablespoon of the crab mixture. Return the baking sheet to the broiler and broil until the crab mixture is heated through and the toasts are browned, about 1 to 2 minutes.

4 Sprinkle with freshly ground black pepper, garnish with the remaining scallions, and serve warm.

Most canned goods stay at peak condition for 3-5 years unopened. Statistically, in an outbreak, canned crab will outlast most survivors.

THAT'S
GONNA STAIN

Trey's pulse quickened at the smear of slime across his hand. He touched his tongue to it. It was the real thing. *Wild blueberries!* Trey felt he had finally found something to make the whole group happy.

They'd been trying to get to Fort Benning for weeks, but the truck was not fast and most of the roads were blocked with abandoned cars. Finally they had run out of gas. With little to eat but Ed's canned spam they were all in a foul mood.

When Trey returned at dusk, Pam quickly mixed a batter from the ripe berries and the last of her precious ingredients. She placed improvised muffin tins in a Dutch oven, and heaped it with hot coals in the fire.

Each of them—except for Earl, who was tied to the truck bumper with the dogs' choke chains—watched the pot in anticipation. Finally Trey had to get up to pee.

Pam was about to call him back when an agonized scream came from behind the truck.

Pam picked up Trey's pizza peel. A biter came around the vehicle from Trey's direction. Pam wheeled and thrust the peel just as Trey had once shown her. Hot brains smeared the side of the truck.

She found Trey on the ground with a gruesome bite wound in his shoulder. Several walkers were tripping over one another to get to him.

"You got to brain me," he gasped. "Pam, I'm so sorry."

A red mist descended over Pam's vision as she attacked the biters. Ronnie had picked up the cleaver and dispatched a corpse in climbing gear as humanely as she could.

Finally, Ronnie fought her way back to Pam, standing vigil over Trey. The walkers just kept coming. She pulled hard at her mother's arm and shouted. They fled their campsite with nothing but the pizza peel, the cleaver, and the clothes on their backs. The walkers followed.

Trey's lifeless eyes reflected the stars, while Earl fidgeted against his chains on the truck's bumper. From the fire, the Dutch oven exuded a warm aroma of fresh muffins.

FALSE SENSE OF SECURITY BLUEBERRY MUFFINS

makes 1½ dozen muffins

Butter or paper liners for muffin tin

12 tablespoons (1½ sticks) unsalted butter, at room temperature

1½ cups sugar

3 large eggs, at room temperature

1½ teaspoons vanilla extract

1 cup buttermilk

2½ cups all-purpose flour

2 teaspoons baking powder

½ teaspoon baking soda

½ teaspoon salt

1 pint fresh blueberries, stemmed

1 Preheat the oven to 350°F. Grease 18 muffin cups or line with paper liners.

2 Using an electric mixer, violently cream the butter and sugar until light and fluffy and subdued, about 5 minutes. Add the eggs one at a time, scraping down the bowl in between additions. Mix in the vanilla and buttermilk.

3 In a separate bowl, sift together the flour, baking powder, baking soda, and salt. With the mixer on low speed, add the flour mixture to the batter and beat until just mixed. Fold in the blueberries with a spatula and be sure the batter is completely mixed.

4 Spoon the batter into the prepared muffin pans, filling each cup just below the top. Bake for 20 to 25 minutes, until the muffins are lightly browned on top and a cake tester comes out clean.

 PRO TIP For a special breakfast treat, these can be made the night before. But who knows if there will be a tomorrow? Hell with it, eat 'em now.

CANTERBURY

Pam ran hard with Ronnie until the walker swarm was far behind them. But what were they running *to*? They had no shelter. What would they eat? How would they cook?

Ronnie stopped dead and looked upward. Out of the morning mist, just behind a line of trees, loomed two crenellated towers. Between them was an open drawbridge with a portcullis.

Pam shook her head in disbelief. "This can't be for real," she said.

"It can be, and it is," said a low voice.

Pam spun around. Behind them stood two men dressed in knights' armor and helmets with visors. One held a rifle on her.

. . .

"What the hell *is* this place?" Pam demanded when their captor removed the blindfold.

They found themselves in a banquet hall right out of medieval times, its walls hung with axes and banners. Half a dozen people in modern dress were calmly setting a long table with pewter plates and mugs, as if for a sumptuous meal. There were armored guards at the door.

"The King will answer your questions," said the man. He removed his armor and helmet to reveal a flannel work shirt and jeans. "For now, you two need to rest. All I can tell you is, you're safe here. We keep the walkers outside, and we lead normal lives inside. At least, as normal as you can when you're shut in a medieval theme restaurant."

A tall, good-looking man strode into the room and whispered to the man who brought them in. He nodded twice and looked closely at Pam.

"Welcome to Canterbury Times," he announced.

Ronnie glared at him as he held out a tray.

"Would my ladies care for a popper?"

SECRETLY SADISTIC JALAPEÑO POPPERS

makes 32 jalapeño poppers

16 large jalapeño peppers, halved lengthwise

8 ounces cream cheese (about 1 cup), at room temperature

4 ounces Jack or sharp Cheddar cheese, shredded (about 1 cup)

⅓ cup fresh or frozen corn kernels

¼ cup minced yellow onion

¼ cup chopped fresh cilantro

1½ teaspoons ground cumin

1 teaspoon chili powder

Pinch of cayenne

1 teaspoon salt

Nonstick spray

Lime wedges, for serving

1 Preheat the oven to 375°F.

2 Using a spoon, carve out the guts, veins, and seeds of the jalapeños. Rinse under cold water to loosen any remaining seeds and let dry hollow side down on paper towels.

3 Meanwhile, prepare the filling. In a small bowl, smash together the cream cheese, shredded cheese, corn, onion, cilantro, cumin, chili powder, cayenne, and salt until smooth.

4 Spray a large rimmed baking sheet with nonstick spray and distribute the jalapeño boats, hollow side up. Depending on the size of the pepper, fill each jalapeño with 1 to 1½ teaspoons of the cheese filling. Bake for 20 to 25 minutes, or until the peppers are tender and the cheese is bubbling and beginning to brown. Squeeze fresh lime juice over the top and serve hot.

Theme restaurants make good hideouts during crises, with their large interior spaces, elaborate food preparation facilities, and defensible facades. But you're better off bringing your own food.

MEDIEVAL TIMES
GONE BYE

Ronnie didn't trust this place. It felt like a school play. It didn't add up. And her mother was falling for it.

"'King'?" she heard her mother ask. "They really call you that?"

"Some nicknames stick whether you want them to or not," he said. "I was head chef. None of the others wanted to make hard decisions or even knew how to cook. I organized the watch, scouted propane for the ovens, and secured ingredients. These people look to me for leadership. If you prefer, you may call me Philippe."

"So what's with the armor?" Ronnie asked.

"It was made for shows at the restaurant, but walkers can't bite through it. I mean, look around. Civilization's been thrown back to the dark ages. Nothing out there but thugs, monsters, and awful food. In here, the men of the watch patrol the area. The mall behind the north door is overrun with walkers, but we haven't had a single casualty inside the restaurant. We've got a vegetable garden on the roof, and we have livestock of sorts. We eat sustainably. We make the Middle Ages thing work for us."

The inhabitants of Canterbury assembled around the large table. Servers brought out large trays of ham and biscuits with steaming coffee. It was more food than Pam and Ronnie had seen in ages.

"You see?" said the King, sitting back in his aluminum throne. "Life as it once was."

Ronnie glowered. Her mother smiled stupidly.

Ronnie poked at the ham on her plate with her fork. She didn't eat animal products, but she knew that this wasn't ham.

The King added, "Hope you'll stay for the show tonight."

Ronnie made a gurgling sound deep in her throat.

DIRE HAM BISCUITS

serves 12

4 tablespoons unsalted butter, softened, plus more
for greasing pan

1 cup sour cream

½ cup whole milk

2 cups self-rising flour, plus more for dusting

1 tablespoon sugar

6 ounces cooked country ham, or any cooked ham, or
any protein you can get your hands on, finely chopped

Orange marmalade, for serving

1   Preheat the oven to 450°F. Lightly grease a baking sheet with butter
or spray with cooking spray.

2   To make the biscuits, in a small bowl or measuring cup, stir together
the sour cream and milk until smooth. In a large bowl, mix together
the flour and sugar. Pour in the sour cream mixture and fold together
until a soft dough forms. Turn the dough out on a surface that's
been lightly sprinkled with extra flour. Knead the dough until it just
comes together.

3   Roll or pat the dough out until it's about ¾ inch thick. Dip a 2-inch
biscuit cutter in flour and cut out the biscuits, placing them at least
1 inch apart on the prepared baking sheet. Bake until golden brown,
10 to 12 minutes, and transfer to a wire rack to cool slightly.

4   While the biscuits are baking, make the ham filling. In a bowl, mix
together the ham and butter until combined. Split the hot biscuits
in half and spread one side thickly with ham butter and the other
with a thin smear of the marmalade, then close them up to make
sandwiches. Serve while they're still warm.

Be wary of snacks offered by strangers. Trust is vital
when sharing food in a world of dodgy food sources.

SWEETBREAD AND
CIRCUSES

A fanfare proclaimed the beginning of the evening's show. The townsfolk of Canterbury crowded into the tiers around the arena at the center of the restaurant.

"Friends, welcome to Medieval Kitchen Stadium," the King announced from his aluminum throne. "Let's meet our challengers!"

From a curtained arch in the side of the arena emerged three men in armor. Behind them, on chains, they dragged six lurching walkers, including a dwarf. They locked the chains to rings in the walls.

"And tonight's secret ingredient..."

Out of the curtain spilled nearly a dozen frolicsome fur-balls.

"Kittens!"

Ronnie gripped the rail in front of her. How could this be happening? "This is barbaric!" she screamed. She stormed out of the arena.

The King seemed taken aback. "We're just letting off a little steam," he said. "Besides," he confided to Pam, "it's fixed. The walkers aren't near quick enough to catch those cats."

It was true. The walkers staggered around after the kittens, who pranced around playfully but kept their distance from the foul-smelling creatures. The townsfolk of Canterbury cheered for their favorites.

But Pam wasn't listening. Her attention was fixed on the dwarf.

"Earl!" she cried.

She jumped up from the table, the pizza peel in her hand.

The men of the watch tried to stop her, but they couldn't keep up in their costume armor. She landed on the sandy floor of the arena and twirled the peel. She brained one walker with the blade and stuck the handle through the rotten skull of the other. The kittens scuttled away as Pam felled each walker in turn except for Earl, who held his good arm out to her. He was ready to feed.

The King scowled. She couldn't be sure, but from the floor Pam thought he said, "Looks like we've got a new secret ingredient."

SECRET-INGREDIENT CHEESE FINGERS

makes 48

1 cup flour

1½ teaspoons baking powder

½ teaspoon salt

⅛ teaspoon ground cayenne pepper

4 tablespoons cold unsalted butter, cut into 8 pieces

½ cup shredded sharp Cheddar cheese

¼ cup grated Parmesan cheese, plus extra for sprinkling

3 tablespoons sour cream, plus more for brushing

1 teaspoon Dijon mustard

1 In a large bowl or in a food processor, stir or pulse together the flour, baking powder, salt, and cayenne. Add the butter, Cheddar, and Parmesan and pulse or cut in with a pastry blender or your fingers until well combined; stir or pulse in sour cream and mustard. Shape the dough into a ball, wrap in plastic, and chill for at least 2 hours. And up to 3 days.

2 Preheat the oven to 425°F. On a lightly floured surface, roll out dough ⅛ inch thick. Cut into fingers ½ inch wide and 3 inches long. Brush each finger with sour cream and sprinkle with more Parmesan cheese.

3 Bake for 7 to 9 minutes, until pale golden brown on top. Serve warm or at room temperature.

 As you prepare the cheese "fingers" pay close attention that no actual fingers get mixed in.

SELF-PRESERVATION

A figure in a black hood melted into the shadows of the castle, away from the barbarous noises of the arena.

This place held a dark secret, Ronnie could sense it. She passed the walled-up entrance to the mall, and descended a staircase to the stillness of the kitchen. The large freezers stood silent and empty. The cupboards contained only dry goods and a few garden vegetables. But there was blood on the floor.

A corridor opened from the side of the kitchen. A long window looked out onto a stable big enough for ten horses. But there were no horses. In their place Ronnie saw a motley collection of small furry animals: guinea pigs, bunnies, kittens, puppies, hamsters, even an aquarium full of goldfish.

OMG cute! It was like a whole pet store had been stashed here in this basement—but why?

The answer awaited next door.

In the tack room next to the stable Ronnie found a wall of shelves arrayed with aquariums. Inside of them, hazy animal forms sat pickling in a cloudy, greenish liquid.

Ronnie drew a breath. She thought tearfully of the "ham."

"So you've found our little secret," someone said behind her, making her nearly jump out of her skin. She backed against the door to the stable as the King approached.

"You wouldn't do any different," he chided. "By the time we finished the horses, the woods were pretty much hunted out by the walkers. The mall had a pet store. In this world, either you eat the pet food or you eat the pets."

"You're sadistic," Ronnie spat.

He smiled uncomfortably. "You have to get it where you can find it. We eat sustainably in Canterbury. It's just, we eat smaller than before."

Ronnie reached for the doorknob to the stable.

GRUESOME TROPHY PICKLED SHRIMPS

makes 1 pound pickled shrimp

1½ cups water

½ cup white vinegar

½ cup apple cider vinegar

1 lemon, zested and juiced

1 fennel bulb, thinly sliced

1 garlic clove, peeled

¾ cup granulated sugar

½ teaspoon whole black peppercorns

1 teaspoon coarse kosher salt

1 pound 16–20 count shrimp, peeled and deveined

2 tablespoons finely chopped parsley

2 tablespoons finely chopped basil

1 tablespoon finely chopped fennel fronds

1 tablespoon finely chopped dill

1 In a large pot over medium-high heat, combine the water, white vinegar, apple cider vinegar, lemon juice, fennel, garlic, sugar, black peppercorns, and salt. Bring to a boil to dissolve the sugar. Add the shrimp and cook, stirring, for 30 seconds. Transfer the shrimp and liquid to a large bowl and cool to room temperature.

2 Stir in the lemon zest, parsley, basil, fennel fronds, and dill. Cover and refrigerate for at least 3 hours, up to overnight.

PRO TIP — Catch or pick food when it's available and preserve it for those times when the living dead make shopping difficult.

THE ONE-EYED KING

No!" shouted the King.

He dived to prevent her, but it was too late. Ronnie had thrown open the stable doors and released the livestock of Canterbury. Puppies and kittens darted out, leading a small stampede of guinea pigs, gerbils, parakeets, and a gecko.

He desperately tried to herd them back into the stable, but Ronnie stuck out her leg. The King tripped and crashed headfirst through the glass of one of the aquariums.

The shelves collapsed, spilling preserved victuals across the room, while the liberated pets scampered across the slippery floor in a panic.

The King fell to the ground and screamed, reaching for an oozing white orb that rolled out of his grasp. "My eye, you put out my eye!"

It was actually a pickled egg, though he had sustained a cut near his right eye. A puppy licked his briny face.

Ronnie fled.

. . .

Pam tied Earl with the choke chain he was still wearing, and led him out of the arena. The knights had run to find the screaming King. No one in this world had honor anymore, or even good sense. She wondered what Daryl would have done. He would have kicked some ass if he was there. But he wasn't. She'd have to do it herself.

She had to find Ronnie. She was going to keep her family together if it killed her.

MEDIEVALED EGGS

makes 24 deviled eggs

1 dozen large eggs, hard cooked and peeled
¼ cup mayonnaise
¼ cup sour cream
2 teaspoons Dijon mustard
1 teaspoon prepared horseradish
Dash or two of hot sauce
Salt and freshly ground black pepper to taste
Paprika, for garnish

1 Halve the eggs lengthwise and pop the yolks out into a medium bowl. Arrange the whites on a serving platter.

2 Mash the yolks with the mayonnaise, sour cream, mustard, horseradish, hot sauce, and salt and pepper to taste until everything is thoroughly combined and smooth.

3 Spoon the filling back into the egg whites and serve them with a dusting of paprika.

A piping bag for the egg filling makes a cheery, pre-outbreak touch. In a pinch, make a piping bag from a pillowcase and a spent shotgun shell.

BEYOND
THE WALL

Pam and Ronnie dragged Earl through the corridors of the castle. The alarm had been raised, and Canterbury was in total disarray.

They found themselves at the mall entrance, where a tall, white wall had been thrown up to keep out the walkers. The men of the watch had deserted it as they scrambled to recapture the freed animals.

"What kind of sick mind pits kittens against the living dead?" Ronnie sobbed.

"The kind this world creates," Pam said. "We might all be better off outside these walls than in."

At that moment the King emerged from the basement, a patch over his wounded eye. He raved at the fugitives. "You won't last a day beyond the wall," he said. "Winter is coming! Winter is coming! The walkers will get you if the savages don't!"

Pam and Ronnie had already torn open the wall and unlatched the glass doors to the mall. They found themselves in a multilevel shopping mall, infested with undead suburbanites.

The King's screaming instantly drew the attention of the walkers. Many staggered toward the breech in the wall, where the men of the watch already had their hands full with the puppies. Others came toward Pam with hungry, dogged steps.

The biters seemed to ignore Ronnie as long as she stayed close to her brother. She held his leash and tried to get him to stop squirming.

Pam had whipped out the pizza peel and started jabbing. Heads went skidding across the mall floor as brains and gore accumulated in a wobbling heap around her.

"Earl, cut it out, you pest!" shouted Ronnie.

Earl's sack had slipped.

"Earl!" she wailed, but it was too late. She fell, her brother's teeth sunk into her neck.

Pam emptied the contents of one last walker's head with the peel and knelt over her daughter, trying uselessly to stanch the wound.

"Ronnie! Ronnie, no!"

"Mother, please," the girl said softly. "It's Nica. Not Ronnie."

GRATUITOUS VIOLENCE JELL-O MOLD

serves 8 to 10

2 cups pomegranate juice, not from concentrate

1 cup sparkling or dry white wine

4 (7¼-ounce) envelopes unflavored gelatin

¼ cup sugar

⅓ cup pomegranate seeds, plus more for garnish

2 (14-ounce) cans sweetened condensed milk

1 cup cottage cheese (optional)

1 In a mixing bowl, combine ½ cup pomegranate juice and the wine. Add the contents of 3 gelatin packets. Fill a large bowl with ice water.

2 In a small saucepan over high heat, bring the remaining juice and sugar to a boil. Stir it into the juice and gelatin mixture. Place the bowl in the ice bath to cool, then transfer the gelatin mixture to the refrigerator until it thickens, 20 to 30 minutes.

3 In a 10-cup Bundt pan, distribute the pomegranate seeds over the bottom. Add the gelatin mixture and return to the fridge for 10 minutes, or until set but still sticky.

4 Meanwhile, in a medium bowl, sprinkle the remaining gelatin over 1 cup cold water and allow it to absorb the water. Stir in 3 cups boiling water for 2 minutes, until gelatin is fully dissolved. Stir in the condensed milk. Chill the mixture in the ice bath and then gently spoon it into the mold over the pomegranate gelatin layer. Refrigerate overnight or until firm.

5 To unmold, fill sink with warm water. Dip the mold just to the rim in the water for 30 seconds. Lift from water, dry the outside with a towel, and loosen the edges of the gelatin from the mold. Place a cold, moistened plate over the top of the mold and invert the plate and mold together. Carefully lift the mold; if gelatin does not release, dip the mold in warm water and try again.

6 Before serving, scoop the cottage cheese into the center of the mold and serve garnished with more pomegranate seeds.

This low-risk dessert makes an arresting presentation, and it's an elegant reminder that another gruesome battle is always just around the corner.

NACHO WORLD
NO MORE

Pam muzzled her teenage daughter with duct tape. Not that she hadn't been tempted many times before, but she never expected to actually have to do it. When your kid turns into a living dead monster, everyone has different ways of coping.

After clearing a section of the mall, she hid her family in a booth at the Chuck E. Cheese's. She wrapped the dog chains around both kids. Then, with exaggerated calm, she improvised a plate of nachos in the kitchen and tried to make sense of her situation.

She still felt like that timid girl hiding behind a tree in the Blue Ridge Mountains. Back then, Daryl had protected her and taught her to use a hatchet in exchange for the best cheese sandwich she knew how to make. Now there was no one to show her what to do and no one to make snacks for but herself.

She tried on Ronnie's hoodie. The silkscreened pink skull felt about right. She strapped Trey's pizza peel to her back using Earl's SpongeBob backpack, and hitched the cleaver in her belt.

Her reflection, glimpsed in a shop window, made her shudder.

She exited the mall, undead children in tow. The hoodie, or else the presence of her biter children, seemed to mask her from the ravenous throng of walkers still clustered there. She relished her invisibility.

In some ways, little had changed. Earl still fidgeted and wandered. Ronnie still rolled her eyes and made that exasperated slurping sound. But at least she wasn't a vegan anymore.

She led them out of the town into the woods. She found a clearing, tied the kids' chains to a tree, and sat down to finish the gooey nachos. It had been their family dish, the one food they could always agree on. Now she'd have to throw in a live field mouse or a squirrel to get them to eat it.

She tried in vain to brush Ronnie's hair, but Ronnie pulled away and made that slurping sound. She felt she hadn't been the best mother. But she wouldn't give up. She would adapt to her kids' special needs, and they would get through this thing as a family.

NACHOS OF THE LIVING DEAD
serves 8

Nonstick spray

1 (13-ounce) bag corn tortilla chips

1 (15-ounce) can refried beans

5 ounces cured (cooked) chorizo, diced small (don't use fresh chorizo here)

½ cup pickled jalapeños

1 pound (4 cups) pepper Jack cheese, grated

Pico de gallo or salsa, for serving

Mexican *crema* or sour cream, for serving

Chopped cilantro, for serving

Lime wedges, for serving

1 Preheat the oven to 425°F.

2 Coat a large rimmed baking sheet with nonstick spray and distribute half of the tortilla chips in a single layer. Dollop half of the refried beans, half of the chorizo, half of the jalapeños, and half of the cheese. Cover with the remaining chips and repeat the process with the remaining ingredients. Bake for 15 to 20 minutes, or until the cheese is melted and beginning to brown.

3 Let nachos cool slightly, then garnish with the pico de gallo, *crema,* cilantro, and lime wedges. Serve on the baking sheet.

Don't worry if you can't find nonstick spray. A chisel works just as well.

FIGHT THE DEAD AND
FEED THE LIVING

A man in an orange fishing vest stumbled, dazed and frantic, through the orchard. The biters had gotten his kids and his wife. Now he was lost, alone, and weak with hunger.

He'd already jumped at so many stray noises that this time he failed to notice the sound of a snapping twig. A willowy woman in a torn mauve pantsuit lunged at him from behind a bush. She had the same starved look in her eye as he probably did. Except she had found something to eat. Him.

He lifted the heavy tire iron he carried in his belt. As he crushed her skull he heard a crunch of leaves. Two more walkers converged on him out of nowhere, grabbing at his shirt and dragging him down. He was too weak to lift the tire iron a second time. He squeezed his eyelids shut and saw a vision of his wife on their wedding day.

There was a whistle like a scythe through grass, a warm rain on his face, and the smell of bacon. He opened his eyes one at a time.

The walkers lay on the ground, the tops of their heads like putrescent bowls dribbling red on the dry leaves.

Above him stood Death.

She wore a black hood that obscured her face, but her sweatshirt was emblazoned with a hot pink skull. She carried some kind of long shovel, its edges filed sharp and smeared with gore. Her left hand gripped two chains, at the ends of which swayed a pair of smallish biters, their mouths sealed with duct tape.

"You must be hungry," said the apparition.

The man's throat dried shut. He nodded.

She held out a cleaver with bacon balanced on its flat. The man gawped at it in wonder.

"Bon appétit," said the specter. "In this world, you either snack or get snacked on."

ANGEL OF DEATH BROWN SUGAR BACON BITES
serves 6 to 8

8 strips bacon, each cut into 3-inch pieces
(about ½ pound)
Nonstick baking spray
¼ cup light brown sugar
¼ teaspoon ground cayenne pepper
½ teaspoon ground cinnamon

1 Preheat the oven to 400°F. Line a baking sheet with aluminum foil
   and add the bacon pieces in a single layer. Line another baking
   sheet with paper towels and place a cooling rack on top. Spray the
   cooling rack with nonstick spray and set aside.

2 In a small bowl, stir together the brown sugar, cayenne, and
   cinnamon. Sprinkle the brown sugar mixture evenly over the bacon
   pieces. Bake until the bacon is well browned, crisp and bubbling,
   16 to 18 minutes. Remove the baking sheet from the oven.

3 Transfer the bacon pieces to the cooling rack and set aside to cool
   completely and firm up before serving.

 PRO TIP Cut these into bite-size pieces for an uncluttered
look and effortless eating. A sensible hand food for
hand-to-hand situations.

TWO
EATING
ON THE RUN

THE CHOPPER

Daryl thundered down the road on his brother's motorcycle, crossbow slung on his back, poncho flapping in the wind, a hatchet handle dangling from his open saddlebag. He was on a mission.

He sped past walkers drawn by the unmuffled engine. One of them stood moronically in the middle of the road. Reaching for the hatchet, he gunned the motor and drove right at the walker. He caught a glimpse in the rear-view mirror of the dead geek's head flying off. He liked the loneliness of the open road.

He'd left the group of survivors to get supplies, but he would have found just about any excuse to get out of there. Their endless debating, finger-pointing, and crazy moods made his insides coil up tight. You can brain a biter, but how do you survive the survivors?

That was the thing that scared him the most. He wasn't sure he was coming back.

People had spooked him his whole life. His parents only yelled or whupped him when they paid him any mind at all, and his brother's protective care wasn't much gentler.

But there had been this one girl he couldn't scare off. She used to bring him cheese sandwiches. There hadn't been much to eat at home, what with his brother Merle gone and his dad sleeping off his liquor most of the time.

He could barely ever manage to say two words to her, but she'd come back every few days with a homemade lunch. He had been just a dumb kid, but he knew an angel when he saw one. First time the wolf in his gut stopped yapping for a second.

She'd asked him to show her how he skinned a squirrel. He'd always used a hatchet; it got less hair in the meat. He had wrapped her pale hand in his on the hatchet handle and guided her arm.

"First you chop the head," he told her. He'd wondered if she noticed how bad his hand was shaking. He couldn't look at her the rest of the day.

Damn, what was that girl's name?

By the end of that summer her family had moved back down near Atlanta, and he'd gone back to roaming the woods alone. He was probably better off on his own. Not like she was his family. The outbreak didn't change a thing.

Of course he knew things weren't the same now. He just wasn't always sure how. Seemed to him the living weren't so different from the dead sometimes. The dead are hungrier is all. And there are a lot more of them.

Up ahead the road ended in a lake. The creek was flooded. Time to hoof it. He found a low mound and hid the Bonneville behind it in vines and poplar. He didn't like to stash his brother's bike like that, but where was his damn brother now?

The living made claims on you the dead couldn't, even if you didn't want them to. The sheriff, the children, the old man, the woman with the secret strength, they'd all lost family. Now they were the only family he had left. He'd do what he could for them.

He tried not to think about it. He grabbed the hatchet, adjusted the crossbow, and started walking.

Daryl was going shopping.

FOOD CHAIN

Hellooo, dinner," Daryl said, shifting the crossbow to his back. He pulled his bolt from where it had stapled the squirrel to a tree.

He tried to remember if he'd cleaned the bolt since the last walker he'd brained. He was sure he had. He sniffed it. Pretty sure.

He hooked the squirrel under his belt and continued east. Without the chopper he'd have to stay off the main road, which was basically a big old biter tailgate party. He'd stick to the woods and fields and parallel Route 16 at least till the river. From there he'd see.

The woods were quiet. No quail, not even a rabbit. Poplar shoots were everywhere, meaning deer hadn't eaten them. He'd seen a half-chewed doe that could've made a good meal if it hadn't been slobbered on by a bunch of dead assholes.

If he couldn't hunt, he'd have to raid houses. There wasn't much between here and the Flint River. He'd make it the rest of the day on squirrel power though.

At dusk he came to a white house, its porch mostly swallowed up by honeysuckle. No car out front. Big propane tank out back. He pushed the back door open and pounded loudly, hiding himself behind the door jamb like a pranking kid.

He gave it a minute. Nothing.

He did a sweep of the house, then tested the oven. Bingo, some propane left in that tank.

The kitchen smelled faintly of paprika. He liked raw squirrel well enough, but there were other ways to fix it, too.

SQUIRREL POPPERS
makes 15 poppers

3 tablespoons unsalted butter

2 cups finely chopped cooked squirrel meat or rotisserie chicken

½ teaspoon sweet paprika

Coarse kosher salt

Freshly ground black pepper

2¼ cups all-purpose flour

¾ cup chicken broth

¼ cup heavy cream

1 tablespoon fresh lemon juice

1 teaspoon paprika

2 teaspoons flaky sea salt

1 tablespoon finely chopped Italian flat-leaf parsley

2 eggs

2 cups bread crumbs or panko

Canola oil

Lemon wedges, for serving

1 In a large skillet set over medium-high heat melt the butter. Add the squirrel or chicken and season with the sweet paprika, salt, and pepper. Stir in ¼ cup of the flour until a smooth paste forms. Gradually whisk in the chicken broth and 3 tablespoons of the cream. Simmer until thickened, about 4 minutes; whisk in lemon juice, then transfer the mixture to a bowl, cover, and chill for at least 1 hour.

2 In a small bowl, use your hand to mix together the paprika, sea salt, and parsley.

PRO TIP

Paprika is a tasty complement for nearly any small woodland creature or urban rodent.

3 Use dampened hands to divide the chicken mixture into 15 balls (about 2 tablespoons each). In a medium bowl, add the remaining flour. In a second medium bowl, whisk together the eggs with 1 tablespoon cream. In a third bowl add the bread crumbs. Dredge each chilled croquette first in the flour, then in the egg, and finally coat the croquettes with bread crumbs and transfer to a plate.

4 Add enough oil to come 1 inch up the sides of a medium saucepan. Heat until shimmering then fry the croquettes in batches until golden brown and heated through, 5 to 7 minutes. Sprinkle with the parsley-paprika sea salt and serve immediately with lemon wedges.

SINCEREST
CONDOLENCES

The house had a tidy air that made him feel every inch an uncivilized redneck. He slept outside on the porch, his hatchet nestled in the crook of his arm.

Next morning he watched as orange butterflies hovered over a big mound of honeysuckle in the yard. He went for a closer look. A hollow eye socket stared back at him through the sweet-smelling blossoms. He shifted a bit of the vine with the tip of his hatchet. He made out a ripped pink floral housecoat, faded almost gray by the seasons. He turned and went back in the house.

The fridge was stocked with mold, tendrils creeping around the door and up the side like fingers. In the freezer were some thawed pizzas slouched in their plastic packaging. Hell, he decided, those things never go bad, and anyway pizza was like beer. When it's good it's real good, and when it's bad it's still pretty good.

He hadn't figured Mrs. Floral Print for the frozen-pizza type. He thanked her silently. He remembered the girl with the sandwiches from when he was a kid. She could make serious vittles out of anything. Once she had pulled a frozen pizza from the permafrost of his dad's freezer and next thing he'd known she'd made a sandwich. She had never seemed to mind, but Daryl knew he hadn't done a thing to deserve it.

He hadn't been able to tell her what he'd been feeling, and even if he had, he'd been afraid of what might come out. Then she had moved away and it was too late. He never saw her again and never got to say good-bye. But her food was a kindness he never forgot.

It started to rain outside. He opened an envelope sitting on the kitchen table. A card.

"Get well soon," it said. He stood it on a shelf.

Better late than never, I guess. But not by much.

He tore into the pizzas.

TURKEY PIZZA CLUBS
makes 2 sandwiches

1 (10-inch) store-bought cheese pizza
4 slices bacon, halved crosswise
2 tablespoons mayonnaise
Freshly ground black pepper
4 butter lettuce leaves
½ tomato, sliced into 4 rounds
¾ pound cooked turkey breast, sliced into 8 slices

1 Bake the pizza according to the package instructions. When just cool enough to handle, slice into four 5-inch by 3-inch squares. (Eat the scraps.)

2 While the pizza is baking, heat a large skillet over medium-high heat. Add the bacon and cook until browned and crisp, 3 to 4 minutes on each side. Transfer to a paper towel–lined plate and set aside to cool.

3 To assemble each sandwich: Arrange 2 pizza slices in a row, cheese side up. Spread each with 1 tablespoon of mayonnaise and season with pepper. Place 2 lettuce leaves on top of the mayonnaise and then top with 2 tomato slices. Layer 2 slices of the bacon over the tomatoes and top with half of the turkey. Carefully top each with the remaining slices of pizza, cheese side down.

4 Use a serrated knife to cut each sandwich, diagonally, into 2 triangular pieces and serve.

 Frozen pizza dough will last long into the outbreak.

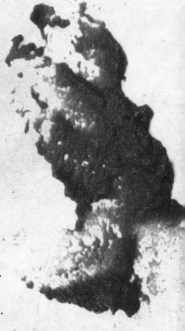

BESIDE THE
DYING FIRE

The rain didn't bother him much, but the chill made him feel more alone. He lit some coals in a barbecue and brought it up to the porch. Fact was, he didn't trust houses. His first house burned down with his mother inside it. Merle eventually fled the next house, leaving him there with a drunk dad who whipped him bloody. He'd take the woods over a house any day.

But a kitchen, that came in handy. His mama hadn't been much of a cook, but the few times she paid him any mind she'd made him a pimento-cheese sandwich. She'd fed it to him and watched him eat. Those were the few times he'd felt warm and safe. His mama's pimento cheese tasted like home.

Thing about a sandwich—you could manage it. You could carry it, it didn't get in your way, and it wouldn't desert you. A sandwich had your damn back.

He was lost in thought when a walker came spilling out of the front door at him like a drunken ape. Must've gotten in the back door. He'd let his guard down.

He jumped back, keeping the Weber between them. The biter's desiccated skin had pulled away from its broken teeth, leaving an obscene grimace.

"Shoulda told me you were coming," he said. "I'd've combed my hair."

The biter stumbled and caught itself on the grill. Coals clung to its arm like nettles, and flames sprang up on its ragged sleeve. It went up like a match.

He gave it a roundhouse kick to the chest, throwing the thing backward into the house. He followed it in with his hatchet. By the time he got near enough to brain it, flames had peppered the tidy old living room.

He grabbed some flour and hot sauce from the kitchen, then stood outside watching the smoke escape through the lace curtains. He felt Mrs. Floral Print would want it this way.

But he had to admit, the smell of singed meat was making him hungry.

BURN-THE-HOUSE-DOWN BBQ SAMMY

makes 10 to 12 servings

PORK

1 tablespoon salt

1 teaspoon garlic powder

½ teaspoon black pepper

½ teaspoon cayenne

¼ teaspoon celery seeds

1 (7-pound) boneless pork shoulder, skin and fat left intact

BASTING SAUCE

3 cups apple cider vinegar

1 cup ketchup

2 tablespoons Worcestershire sauce

2 tablespoons dry mustard powder

2 tablespoons packed dark brown sugar

2 teaspoons crushed red pepper flakes

2 teaspoons salt

1 teaspoon chili powder

½ teaspoon black pepper

Hot sauce, to taste (optional)

10 to 12 soft buns

Shredded cabbage or lettuce

1 At least 12 hours and up to 3 days ahead, start the pork. In a small bowl, combine the salt, garlic powder, black pepper, cayenne, and celery seeds. Rub the spice mixture all over the pork to coat evenly. Place pork in a covered bowl and refrigerate overnight.

2 Combine all sauce ingredients in a large saucepan and stir to dissolve the sugar. Let simmer for 3 minutes, then let cool. Store in the refrigerator for up to a week.

3 Preheat the oven to 300°F and place a rack inside a large roasting pan. Transfer the pork to the rack and bake for 2½ hours, then pour half the sauce over the pork and continue to bake 1 to 2 hours more, basting pork every 30 minutes with sauce and drippings from bottom of the roasting pan. When done, the internal temperature of the meat should register 180°F.

4 Remove the pork from the oven and let cool on the rack until cool enough to handle. Meanwhile, warm the remaining sauce in a sauce-pan over low heat. Transfer the warm pork to a cutting board and shred, pull, tear, and chop the meat into bite-size pieces, mixing in some of the fat and skin. Transfer pork to a large bowl; add sauce to taste, and mix to combine. Season with hot sauce to taste if you like.

5 Serve the pork on buns with cabbage or lettuce, passing any remaining sauce on the side.

PRO TIP

A portable grill should be on your go-list. Fuel is easy to make yourself, and the hot coals are less likely than a campfire to attract drop-in dinner guests.

OUT OF THE BAG

He followed a line of uneven footprints in the undergrowth, his brother's Marine knife in his hand. The knife had gotten Merle into trouble oftener than out of it, but it was sharp and could drop a walker quick enough.

Years ago, after Merle had left home for good, Daryl had stolen his brother's old BB gun and taken off into the woods.

He hadn't known what he was going to do with it. He didn't even have hair on his face yet. He ran till he tasted blood in his mouth. He wanted to be alone, far from his dad's brutal temper.

He fixed a scampering critter in the gun sight and fired. Just a damn squirrel. In his mind he could hear his brother laughing at him. But by now he was hungry.

He laid the animal belly-up on a fallen log. He opened it up with his hatchet and started to eat.

A twig snapped. He spun around to see a scruffy girl staring at him from behind a tree. She didn't look as scared as he felt. He yelled at her to get the hell out of here.

She just kept looking at him. His cheeks burned and he closed up the squirrel to hide its exposed insides. He wiped at a drop of blood running down his chin.

Finally, she asked him for the squirrel.

He didn't know what to do. He squinted at her and held out the dripping carcass. She took it from him and ran off, holding the animal at arm's length. His brother would have laughed his ass off. But he never told his brother.

Next day she found him in the same woods. Without a word she offered him a paper bag. Inside was a hamburger on a bun with fixins. Well, sort of a hamburger. He recognized the taste. But it tasted better than any squirrel he'd had before.

Now he snuck up on a fat walker wearing a fluorescent hunter's vest. He pulled its head back and drove the knife up through its chin, skewering it like a camo kebob.

Hell if he was going to end up like that old squirrel.

WHATCHA GOT CHIPOTLE CHEESEBURGERS

serves 4

¼ cup mayonnaise

1 chipotle chile, minced

2 pounds ground whatever you've got (beef, turkey, lamb, pig, hamster)

Salt and freshly ground black pepper

½ cup (2 ounces) grated Cheddar or Monterey Jack cheese

4 hamburger buns

Lettuce, tomatoes, pickled jalapeños, as you like, for serving

1   Light the grill or heat up your grill pan. In a small bowl, stir together the mayonnaise and chile.

2   Divide the meat into four patties and season well with salt and pepper. Grill burgers until done to taste, 2 to 4 minutes per side. When the burgers are 30 seconds away from being done, top each with a quarter of the cheese. Let cheese melt, then transfer burgers to a plate.

3   Grill the buns on their cut sides until golden, about 1 minute. Serve burgers in the toasted buns topped with the chipotle mayo and lettuce, tomatoes, and/or pickled jalapeños as you like.

 If you just call it a burger, no one has to know what you put in it.

YOU NEED A
MESS OF HELP TO STAND ALONE

It looked like a damn county fair had crossed this field. The grass was trampled, the mud was churned. The tracks were cluttered and confused. He knew there weren't enough survivors left around here to make a mess like this.

He could handle a lot of walkers, but the sheer size of this herd made him hesitate. Must have been anywhere from sixty to a hundred. And they were headed the same direction he was.

He slowed up and decided to look for a place to stop for the night. He risked a fire before the sun set. He took the flour he'd saved and made tortillas. A few dozen dead douchbags sure as hell weren't going to keep him from dinner.

There was no way he could tackle this without help. He still had a woodchuck tucked in his belt. He silently thanked Mrs. Floral Print for the flour and Tabasco.

It was gonna take a lot of hot sauce to face that many biters.

BACKWOODS BURRITO

makes 4 burritos

GROUND BEEF

1 tablespoon olive oil

1 pound ground beef

2 teaspoons cumin

1 teaspoon ground cayenne

Coarse kosher salt

Freshly ground black pepper

1 cup beef stock or water

SMASHED BLACK BEANS

1 tablespoon olive oil

1 garlic clove, finely chopped

1 (15.5-ounce) can black beans, drained and rinsed

2 chipotle peppers packed in adobo, finely chopped

2 tablespoons canned adobo sauce

4 tablespoons water

1 lime, zested and juiced

Coarse kosher salt

Freshly ground black pepper

BURRITOS

4 large flour tortillas

2 cups thinly sliced iceberg lettuce

1 cup fresh cilantro leaves

1 avocado, thinly sliced

1½ cups crumbled queso fresco

Sour cream, for serving

Salsa, for serving

1 Prepare the beef: In a large skillet over medium-high heat add the oil and heat until shimmering. Add the beef and season with cumin, cayenne, salt, and pepper. Cook until the meat is browned, 5 minutes, then stir in the stock and bring to a simmer. Cook until the liquid evaporates, 8 to 10 minutes.

2 Prepare the black beans: In a large skillet over medium-high heat add the oil and garlic and cook until the garlic is fragrant, about 1 minute. Stir in the black beans, chipotle peppers, adobo sauce, water, and lime zest and juice. Cook, violently pummeling the beans with the back of a wooden spoon until the liquid evaporates and the beans are crushed but not yet a paste. Season with salt and pepper.

3 Assemble the burritos: On a clean work surface, lay out the tortillas. Working one at a time place ½ cup of the shredded lettuce in the center of each tortilla. Top with ¼ cup of cilantro, a quarter of the beef, a quarter each of the smashed beans, avocado slices, and queso fresco. Fold in the sides of the tortilla and roll it up, enclosing the filling inside. Serve the burritos with sour cream and salsa.

PRO TIP

It has not been clinically proven, but anecdotal evidence indicates that regular consumers of hot sauce are less palatable to the living dead.

WHEN THE DEAD COME SNACKING

He knew there couldn't be anything still alive on this sad old farm, but he was too hungry not to check. If any chickens had survived this long, they weren't going to survive much longer.

Daryl cut through the plastic poultry netting around the chicken run and skulked up the ramp to the coop door. He nudged it lightly with the hatchet. All quiet, nothing but a bunch of old feathers and dried-out eggs.

Then from under the roosts he heard a sucking sound. A bluish hand shot out from under the lowest tier and grabbed his ankle. He chopped at it with the hatchet and ran out of the coop, the severed hand still clutching his boot heel.

A biter in Carhartts and rubber boots rolled out of the coop and unsteadily gained its feet again. Daryl had dropped the hatchet and was hopping on one foot to remove the twitching hand from his boot. The biter lunged.

He had expected that, and had just enough time to load and fire a crossbow bolt between its crazed eyes. What he didn't expect was the other walker that had sneaked through the tear he'd made in the plastic netting.

Daryl grabbed the new biter's shoulders, spinning it and winding it up in the loose fencing. The more it struggled, the tighter the netting got.

He took a moment to watch the biter struggle like a big angry burrito. Then he grabbed the hatchet and split its face.

No chicken tonight. But he could smell the river nearby, and the poultry netting gave him an idea.

FAST AND FURIOUS FRIED CHICKEN WRAP

makes 4 wraps

RANCH DRESSING

¼ cup buttermilk or plain yogurt

½ cup mayonnaise

2 tablespoons finely chopped fresh chives

2 tablespoons finely chopped fresh Italian flat-leaf parsley

1 tablespoon fresh lemon juice

⅛ teaspoon onion powder

¼ teaspoon kosher salt

2 teaspoons freshly ground black pepper

FRIED CHICKEN

1 pound skinless, boneless chicken thighs, halved crosswise

1½ teaspoons kosher salt

1½ cups all-purpose flour

½ teaspoon cayenne pepper

1 tablespoon freshly ground black pepper

1 cup buttermilk

Peanut or vegetable oil (for frying)

WRAPS

4 (8-inch) sandwich wraps

8 butter lettuce leaves

8 halved cherry tomatoes

1 Prepare the dressing: In a medium bowl, whisk together the buttermilk, mayonnaise, chives, parsley, lemon juice, onion powder, salt, and pepper. Cover and refrigerate until ready to use.

2 Prepare the chicken: Season chicken with 1 teaspoon of the salt. In a medium bowl, whisk together the flour, cayenne, black pepper, and ½ teaspoon of the salt. Pour the buttermilk into another medium bowl. Working with 1 piece at a time, dredge the chicken in the flour mixture and shake off any excess flour. Dip the thighs in the buttermilk, allowing the excess to drip back into the bowl. Dredge again in the flour mixture, shaking off the excess, and transfer to a clean baking sheet.

3 Pour enough oil into a large heavy pot to come 3 inches up the sides and heat over medium heat until a deep-fry thermometer registers 350°F. Line a baking sheet with paper towels and set a wire rack on top. Fry the chicken in batches until golden brown and cooked through, turning the pieces halfway through, about 6 minutes total. Use a spider or slotted spoon to transfer the chicken to the rack.

4 Assemble the wraps: Lay the wraps out on a work surface. Top each wrap with some of the butter lettuce leaves, the tomatoes, and fried chicken. Drizzle each with 2 tablespoons of the dressing. Fold in the short sides of each wrap and roll up like a burrito, enclosing the fried chicken inside. Serve.

PRO TIP

"Wrapping" is a kitchen skill that transfers well to fighting the undead. Rolled in a rug, sheet, or flexible fencing, your assailant will be unable to move, leaving you free to brain it on your own schedule.

LIVE BAIT

A **man could keep going on squirrel sushi only so long.** Daryl was nearing the limit.

He had finally reached the banks of the Flint. He could either swim it or go south to cross at the bridge, but it was getting late and he had to plan for breakfast.

He took a few feet of poultry netting he'd saved from the farm and stitched it into the shape of a pillow with some twine. He left narrow open funnels at each corner. He placed the last of the squirrel guts inside, and sank the thing at a slight angle into the shallows by the river. He wrapped himself in his poncho and hoped for the best.

There was an audible sloshing sound long before he saw them in the predawn darkness. Three shambling shadows making slow progress along the shallows. They were about to stomp all over his trap.

He sighed and got out his hatchet to defend his breakfast. He wheeled around the tree and chopped the lead walker. Too late he realized his mistake. There were at least a dozen walkers behind the first three, one right after the other like a chow line.

He swung the hatchet in a wide arc to win himself a little space. He caught one of them in the head, but the hatchet stuck hard into a tree trunk he hadn't seen properly.

In the darkness one of the biters got the drop on him, pushing him forward. The hatchet pulled loose from the tree as he fell and its blade caught the meat of his calf. He bellowed angrily as he rose back out of the water and rained the hatchet down on the remaining biters until nothing moved. He dragged himself back to his camp to rest.

The sun rose an hour later and he limped back to pull his trap. It was filled up with a plate's worth of red, brownish, and pink crawfish. There was even a blue one.

He figured he probably got twice as many because of his blood in the water. A mudbug will eat anything, and anything will eat him.

Well, almost anything. Even a crawfish won't eat walker meat, and the walkers weren't after his crawfish.

They'd never know what they were missing.

CREEPING CRAWFISH ÉTOUFFÉE TOASTS

serves 4

2 tablespoons vegetable oil

2 tablespoons unsalted butter

1 medium onion, chopped

½ cup chopped celery

½ cup chopped green bell pepper

1 garlic clove, finely chopped

2 tablespoons all-purpose flour

2 cups low-sodium chicken broth

1 tablespoon tomato paste

1 teaspoon Cajun seasoning

2 bay leaves

½ teaspoon hot sauce, or to taste

1 pound peeled crawfish tails, thawed if frozen (or substitute small peeled shrimp)

Salt and freshly ground black pepper to taste

Toast, for serving

¼ cup chopped scallion, for garnish

1 In a large saucepan, heat the oil and butter over medium heat. Add the onion, celery, and bell pepper and cook, stirring occasionally, until very soft, about 10 minutes. Add the garlic and cook for 30 seconds. Add the flour and cook, stirring constantly, for 1 minute. Add the broth, tomato paste, Cajun seasoning, bay leaves, and hot sauce and cook, stirring, until slightly thickened, about 5 minutes. Add the crawfish or shrimp and simmer gently, uncovered, for 10 minutes. Season the étouffée with salt and pepper to taste. Remove and discard the bay leaves.

2 Serve the étouffée spooned onto hot toasts and garnished with the scallion.

PRO TIP

If you can't scavenge bread, this is just as tasty over rice—nature's perfect bunker food.

PLAN BEE

He limped alongside Wildcat Creek away from the river. He reached a road and saw a handmade sign: "Grumpy's BBQ."

Just next to the bridge was a cramped old rib shack with a corrugated tin roof. Inside were the remains of maybe five diners around a picnic table. The shriveled jerky that remained of their meals lay untouched on yellowed paper plates.

"Guess they weren't the only ones who showed up for ribs," he said to himself.

A high buzzing sound issued from the back room. He spotted a jagged hole in the wall, bees passing in and out of it.

Finally, he could do something about the nasty gash in his leg.

He tied a bandanna around his face. His reflection in the mirrored beer sign looked like a bank robber. He gathered his poncho tightly around him and draped his head with a screen cut from the window.

He sliced the tops off some beer cans, then filled them with twigs and lit them. When the room had filled with smoke, he set to work.

He cut out a large section of the wall around the hole with his hatchet. From the exposed joist hung an enormous sheet of honeycomb, filling the space between the old wood studs.

The bees buzzed around threateningly despite the smoke. He knew they could sense fear, so he kept his cool.

He picked up one of the smoking cans and held it under the comb. Bees calmed and dropped harmlessly out of it. He heated his knife on the hot twigs and carefully sliced a section of the comb free with the warmed blade.

Then he ran back to the creek, clutching the comb and coughing his lungs inside out. He mashed the comb over the screen with the knife hilt, filling an empty sauce jar from the BBQ place with the pale honey.

He slathered the livid cut in his leg with the antiseptic honey and breathed a little easier.

There was plenty left over to cook up some lunch. But first he had a couple dozen stingers to scrape out of his arms.

LAST STAND SKILLET CORNBREAD WITH HONEY BUTTER

makes 6 to 8 servings

CORNBREAD

1 cup yellow cornmeal

⅔ cup all-purpose flour

1 tablespoon baking powder

1¼ teaspoons salt

1 cup sour cream

½ cup whole milk

⅓ cup honey

2 large eggs

¼ teaspoon baking soda

8 tablespoons (1 stick) unsalted butter

⅓ cup corn kernels, thawed if frozen (optional)

HONEY BUTTER

½ cup (1 stick) softened butter

1 to 2 tablespoons honey, to taste

Few drops fresh lemon juice, to taste

1 Preheat the oven to 375°F.

2 In a large bowl, whisk together the cornmeal, flour, baking powder, and salt. In another bowl, whisk together the sour cream, milk, honey, eggs, and baking soda. Gently fold the wet ingredients into the dry ones until just combined.

3 Place a 9-inch cast-iron skillet over high heat until hot. Melt the butter in the skillet, swirling the pan to coat the bottom and sides with butter. Pour the butter into the batter and stir to combine. Stir in the corn kernels if using. Scrape the batter into the skillet.

4 Bake until the top is golden and a toothpick inserted into the center comes out clean, 25 to 30 minutes.

5 Meanwhile, prepare the honey butter. In a small bowl, mix together the butter, honey, and lemon juice. Serve cornbread warm, slathered with honey butter.

PRO TIP Save your heavy cast-iron pans for small groups of undead. For braining larger packs or swarms, lighter pans or chef's knives will prevent muscle soreness later.

A
WALKING SHADOW

It seemed to him the wood began to move.

On the hill above where he sat by the creek the line of trees teemed with walkers. Not just with one walker, and not a pack, but a swarm that didn't end, like someone had evicted a cemetery.

Well, I'll die with my bolts used up.

When Daryl was little, an old man up the road had kept bees. He'd spied the man, "robbing" the hive a couple of times every summer, digging sourwood honeycomb from the hollowed gum stump out back of his field. The old buzzard wasn't one for sharing.

One day his brother Merle had dared him to get some. Daryl had watched the old man enough to know not to fight or swat when you approached the bee hive, and the bees pretty much laid off him at first.

But when he pulled back the cover the bee swarm rose against him as a single cloud of stingers. His brother laughed and laughed as he scuttled back through the woods, but he stopped laughing when he saw he hadn't let go of the comb. He was a month healing up from the stings.

It had been worth the stings. Mountain honey, thick and raw, was better than any food he'd ever tasted. Besides, it shut Merle up.

Daryl measured the walker swarm's approach. Armed with knife and hatchet, he plunged in where the biters were thinnest. His leg slowed him down, and the walkers flailed at him like he was entering hell through a car wash.

He lost his footing on a wet slope and slid headlong into a deep, muddy swale. A couple walkers tobogganed down after him. He stabbed their heads as they sluiced by. He scrambled up the far side where the walkers' rigid limbs couldn't climb. With a glance back at the godawful horde, he continued eastward along the creek, torn and limping.

The swarm had nearly got him. But he still had his jar of honey.

SWARM BAIT FRIED PB&H'S

makes 4 sandwiches

8 slices white Pullman-style bread
½ cup peanut butter (not unsalted)
6 teaspoons honey
3 tablespoons unsalted butter

1 Spread each of 4 slices of the bread with 2 tablespoons of peanut
   butter. Drizzle each of these slices with 1 teaspoon of honey, and then
   sandwich with the other bread slices.

2 In a large nonstick skillet over medium-high heat, melt 1½ tablespoons
   of the butter. Let the pan heat for 30 seconds and then add 2 of the
   sandwiches. Fry for 2 to 3 minutes, or until golden brown, and then
   flip and cook for an additional 1 to 2 minutes to brown the other
   side. Transfer sandwiches to a plate and repeat the process with the
   remaining butter and sandwiches. Halve the sandwiches on a diagonal
   and serve drizzled with the remaining 2 teaspoons of honey.

PRO TIP Honey is antiseptic and keeps for centuries. You can
bring crystallized honey back to liquid by warming it
by the fire, as long as you're sure there aren't any
walkers nearby.

BALLS IN THE ROUGH

The creek continued under a chain-link fence and he followed it out of the woods, dazed and near dead, and soon found himself in a long clearing overgrown with Bermuda grass. He could make out a large building with a tall portico on the other side. He needed to rest.

There was a loud crack behind him. His face had already hit the grass before he figured out something hard had hit him in the skull.

He woke tied to a stainless-steel table in a large kitchen. He could feel a knot the size of a meatball in the back of his head. Should've known better than to walk onto a damn golf course. He looked around for his knife and his crossbow, but they were gone.

A tall man in a bloodstained pink polo entered the room, followed by a small woman in grass-stained chinos. The man glared at him.

"What the hell hit me?" groaned Daryl.

"I tapped you with a putter," the man said. "You're lucky I didn't use a nine iron."

"You better next time, if you're thinking of taking another shot."

"You looked like a walker."

"You came about that close to making me one."

"What do you want here?" asked Pink Polo. "Who are you?"

"Nobody. I'm just passing through. And I don't need anything from you people, except my crossbow back." He caught a whiff of something grilling. "Well, I wouldn't say no to something to eat."

"We bagged a feral hog near the eighteenth hole just before we caught you. We can spare a meatball, but then you're out of here."

"What the hell is this place?"

"Spalding Country Club. And unless you have pepper flakes on you, it's members only."

The last place in the dying world he wanted to be was a country club. But that hog smelled good.

Just then they heard shouting from outside. And then screaming.

Daryl muttered, "Must've forgotten to mention the biter swarm coming up behind me."

GORY RED GRINDER

makes 4 grinders

MEATBALLS

1 pound ground pork

2 large eggs

⅔ cup panko (Japanese bread crumbs)

¼ cup finely shredded pecorino Romano cheese

¼ cup finely shredded Parmesan cheese

2 tablespoons finely chopped basil

¼ teaspoon red pepper flakes

1 garlic clove, finely chopped

Coarse kosher salt

Freshly ground black pepper

3 tablespoons olive oil

RED SAUCE

1 tablespoon olive oil

1 garlic clove, crushed

1 (28-ounce) can crushed tomatoes

1 small bunch fresh basil

¼ teaspoon red pepper flakes

Coarse kosher salt

Freshly ground black pepper

1 (24-inch) sesame Italian loaf, halved horizontally

1 garlic clove, halved

8 ounces fresh mozzarella, sliced

½ cup fresh basil leaves

¼ cup Parmesan cheese

Red pepper flakes are a better choice than black pepper in your go-kit. They retain their heat longer and you don't need to carry a pepper mill.

1 Prepare the meatballs: In a medium bowl combine the pork, eggs, panko, pecorino, Parmesan, basil, red pepper flakes, garlic, salt, and pepper. Use your hands to mix just to combine then form into 8 large meatballs.

2 Heat the oil in a large, deep skillet over medium-high heat. Add the meatballs and sear until golden on all sides, 8 to 10 minutes. Transfer the meatballs to a plate.

3 Prepare the red sauce: Add the olive oil and garlic to the same pan. Cook until the garlic is fragrant, 1 minute. Add the tomatoes, basil, red pepper flakes, salt, and pepper and cook, stirring, until the sauce thickens slightly, about 10 minutes. Add the meatballs and cook until the meatballs are cooked through and the sauce is thick, 15 minutes.

4 Assemble the grinders: Preheat the broiler. Rub the cut sides of the sesame loaf with the garlic clove and place on a baking sheet. Broil until the bread is toasted, about 2 minutes. Top the bottom half of the bread with the meatballs and sauce and layer mozzarella slices on top. Return to the broiler and broil until the mozzarella melts, 1 to 2 minutes. Sprinkle with basil leaves and Parmesan, top with the top slice of sesame loaf, and cut into 4 sandwiches. Serve hot.

GROUND ROUND

"The fence is down!"

The man in the pink polo rushed out of the kitchen with his putter, leaving Daryl tied to the table. Daryl yanked hard at the ropes until they frayed on the steel edge and came loose.

He hobbled to the door to see what was going on.

Outside a battle was raging. A section of the chain-link fence had been pushed down, and a filthy mob of walkers poured onto the shaggy lawn. The club members were hacking at them with whatever they could find. Wedges and drivers seemed to work best, but not good enough because they were quickly driven back against the giant grill where the hog was already starting to scorch.

He searched the kitchen for his weapons, and found his things piled on a golf bag full of sharpened clubs. He rubbed the bruise on his skull.

Not many of the biters had come around to the front side of the clubhouse yet. He made for the creek as fast as his hurt leg would carry him.

A terrific mechanical roar came from the building behind him. Out of a double garage rumbled a huge riding mower, four whirling blades extended in front of it. The driver waved his hat like a rodeo cowboy and steered the juggernaut straight for the biter swarm.

Biter after biter fell underneath the grinding blades as the man whooped and yelled. But eventually the blades clogged up and the motor sputtered out. Before he could restart it, the doomed driver was pulled down from the cab into the grinding mob of dead, joining his fellow country club members.

Turning his back to the awful sight, Daryl spat, put his crossbow over his shoulder, and limped away to the road.

SLOPPY JOSÉ (OR WHOEVER ELSE)

makes 4 sloppy josés

2 teaspoons olive oil

1 medium yellow onion, finely chopped

1 garlic clove, finely chopped

1 pound ground beef

Coarse kosher salt and freshly ground black pepper

1 (15-ounce) can tomato purée

2 chipotle peppers in adobo, finely chopped

1 lime, juiced

1 teaspoon Worcestershire sauce

½ teaspoon ground cumin

10 cilantro sprigs

1 small white or red onion, coarsely chopped

4 sesame buns, split and toasted

1   Heat a large skillet over medium-high heat, then add the oil. Stir in the yellow onion and garlic and sauté until tender, about 7 minutes. Add the beef and season with salt and pepper. Cook, stirring, until the beef is browned and cooked through, about 8 minutes. Drain off most of the fat and stir in the tomato purée, chipotle peppers, lime juice, Worcestershire, cumin, and half the cilantro sprigs. Cook, stirring occasionally, until thickened, about 20 minutes. Discard the cilantro sprigs.

2   Finely chop the remaining cilantro and add to a small bowl. Mix in the white onion. Serve the sloppy Josés on toasted buns topped with the onion-cilantro mixture.

PRO TIP   Manual meat grinders are well worth the small amount of extra weight. Ground meats are hard to identify, and unusual proteins easier to disguise.

A
POOR BOY A LONG WAY FROM HOME

A **monstrous form rose up in the silent water of the creek.** Daryl fired the crossbow.

"Boo-yah!"

He reeled in the line attached to the bolt, which had impaled a big old flathead catfish. He pulled it up the bank and licked his chops. He still had bread he'd swiped from the country club kitchen.

As he fixed his lunch he wondered what had happened to the girl from the woods with the sandwiches. Maybe she'd grown up and had kids of her own. But what was the point thinking about all that now? The walkers had erased that world.

One day he'd told her about the chupacabra, how it roamed the countryside feeding on live sheep. She told him the story scared her. He picked a wildflower from the side of the creek and gave it to her.

"Ain't no chupacabra gonna get through me," he had promised her. "I'll always protect you."

A low sound came from the trees, interrupting his reverie. It was too loud to be a live killer and too quiet to be a dead one. Maybe it was just his stomach growling.

A pair of miserable eyes met his through the scope. He lowered the weapon. Just a goddamned half-starved dog with a desperate growl. The thing was bone-skinny and stared at his lunch with hungry eyes.

Ah hell, he thought. *Might be some company, though.*

He cut his sandwich in half and tossed it over. The dog snapped it up and swallowed it before it even landed. It stared at him again.

"Don't even think you're getting this half, you mangy dirtbag," he said. The dog whimpered.

He cooked up another sandwich to share and they ate their fill. He called her Charlie after Chuck Norris. Even though she was a girl dog, he felt better having an action hero by his side.

The dog lay down in the leaves beside him and kept watch while exhaustion finally caught up with him.

POSTAPOCALYPTIC PO'BOY

serves 6

Vegetable oil, for frying

2 cups shredded cabbage

⅓ cup mayonnaise

¼ cup thinly sliced red onion

1 teaspoon fresh lemon juice

Salt and freshly ground black pepper

½ cup (1 stick) unsalted butter

2 garlic cloves, smashed and peeled

2 loafs long French or Italian breads (about 14 inches each)

6 (6-ounce) mild white fish fillets such as catfish or tilapia

1 cup buttermilk

1 large egg

1 cup cornmeal

½ cup all-purpose flour

Pinch cayenne

Sliced pickles

Hot sauce, for serving

Lemon wedges, for serving

1 Pour about 3 inches of oil in a deep fryer or large, heavy pot and heat to 375°F. Preheat the broiler.

2 In a bowl, toss together the cabbage, mayonnaise, red onion, lemon juice, salt, and pepper to taste.

3 Melt the butter in a small saucepan over medium-low heat. Add the garlic and cook for 1 minute. Brush the insides of the bread with the garlic butter and broil, cut side up, for about 2 minutes, until the bread turns lightly golden at the edges. Transfer to a rack to cool.

4 Season both sides of the fish fillets with a fair amount of salt and pepper. In a shallow bowl, mix the buttermilk and egg together and season with salt and pepper. In another shallow bowl (or pie plate) mix together the cornmeal, flour, cayenne, salt, and pepper. Dip the fish first in the buttermilk, then dredge in the cornmeal mixture, being sure to cover the fillets completely.

5 Gently drop the fish in the hot oil and fry in batches until the fillets are golden, about 3 minutes; drain on a paper towel–lined platter or paper bag. Sprinkle with salt while the fillets are still hot.

6 To assemble the sandwich, lay the pickles on the bottom half of the bread, then top with fried fish. Spoon a small mound of the cabbage on top of the catfish and close up the sandwich with the remaining bread. Cut each loaf into thirds and serve with hot sauce and lemon on the side.

PRO TIP

In desperate times you can reuse your cooking oil. When the oil cools down, repack it in its bottle before you de-camp.

THE
WOLF INSIDE

Muffaletta!" came a call far off in the woods.

The dog perked her ears and bolted away toward the call.

Daryl unslung the crossbow and followed as fast as he could. If somebody was trying to ring a biter dinner bell, they were doing a great job. It kind of made him hungry too.

"Muffy!" called the voice again. Then a scream.

He followed the clamor to a fallow field. Charlie stood beside a wisp of a woman with long hair and spandex pants, and was barking at the four biters in leather jackets who surrounded them. They all made that sickening slurping noise, except two who were muffled inside their motorcycle helmets. Charlie growled as the woman tried to hold her back.

One of them grabbed the woman by the arm but couldn't do much damage through its biker gloves and helmet. She twisted away with strength that surprised Daryl, but she lost her balance and hit her head on a large rock.

He shouted to draw the walkers away. He fired the crossbow at the one in front but the bolt just bounced off its helmet.

He reloaded and got a bare-headed one through the ear. The biters in the brain buckets came at him, though he didn't know what they thought they were going to do to him with their heads all bottled up like that. He pushed one's head up and drove the knife up through its chin, then took the other's head off with the hatchet. He left the head to roll in the drainage ditch, gurgling harmlessly behind its tinted visor.

When he looked up to deal with the last walker, the wispy woman had already taken the top off its head with a machete.

Charlie looked from the spandex lady to him, panting happily.

"Muffaletta, let's go home," she said weakly to the dog.

"This is your dog?" he asked her, squinting.

The woman touched her hand to her head. It came away bloody. Daryl caught her just before she fell.

THREAT-LEVEL MUFFALETTA

serves 4

¼ cup finely chopped roasted bell peppers

1 tablespoon finely chopped peperoncini peppers

8 kalamata olives, pitted and finely chopped
(1 tablespoon)

2 teaspoons finely chopped capers

1 garlic clove, finely chopped

2 tablespoons red wine vinegar

1 tablespoon olive oil

Coarse kosher salt

Freshly ground black pepper

One 8-inch round bread loaf, sliced in half horizontally
and hollowed out slightly

¼ pound thinly sliced ham

¼ pound sliced mortadella

¼ pound sliced provolone cheese

¼ pound thinly sliced Genoa salami

1   In a small bowl, stir together the bell peppers, peperoncini peppers,
    olives, capers, garlic, vinegar, and olive oil. Season with salt and
    pepper.

2   Spread the pepper mixture over both halves of the bread. Starting
    with the hollowed out bottom loaf, layer the ham, mortadella,
    provolone, and salami. Top with the top half and press down to
    smash the two halves together. Wrap the entire loaf tightly in plastic
    wrap and weight down with a heavy skillet. Refrigerate for at least
    1 hour, up to 1 day.

3   When ready to serve, slice the muffaletta into 4 equal pieces and
    serve.

 Create layers of flavor and texture with whatever you can
loot or hunt. Be resourceful, since almost none of the
traditional ingredients will exist long after the outbreak.

EAT, PREY, LOVE

The woman in spandex leaned more heavily on his shoulder than **Daryl thought strictly necessary.** Charlie-Muffaletta seemed to know where they were going and pranced on ahead.

They reached a road and he soon saw a passenger van and five women. The women jumped up when they saw the trio approaching.

"Maria, what the hell?" said a woman with prayer beads clutched in her fist. She stared at Daryl.

"She was attacked," he told her. "But she wasn't bit."

Maria spandex's friends looked relieved and thanked him till his cheeks flushed. They tended to Maria's head but gave particular attention to his nearly healed calf with their first aid kit. They all found some excuse to touch his leg.

"When the outbreak started," the woman with the beads told him, "we were on a yoga retreat up near Chattahoochee. Guided meditation every day, no phones or radio. When we finally heard what was happening we jumped in the van with Maria's dog and came home as fast as we could. But it took weeks to get through the chaos, and by the time we arrived the town was overrun."

"You survived this long, just the six of you ladies?" he said.

"Yoga makes us strong," said the bead lady.

"Also," said another, "we looted a gun store." She held up a semi-automatic.

"We're heading for Fort Benning. We heard there's still army there."

"Yeah, we like soldiers," said the woman with the gun.

The women stared at him a little too closely. He looked at his shoes.

"Well, I better get on," he said after a pause. "You take good care of that dog."

The bead lady looked disappointed.

"Have a little food before you go," she said. "Maybe you can help a gal out with her fuel pump?"

SURVIVALIST HERO

serves 4

¼ cup mayonnaise

1 tablespoon prepared fresh horseradish

1 teaspoon fresh lemon juice

Coarse kosher salt

Freshly ground black pepper

One 24-inch French bread loaf with sesame seeds, halved lengthwise

2 cups thinly sliced romaine lettuce (about 1 head)

¾ pound sliced turkey

¼ pound sliced Swiss cheese

¾ pound sliced ham

¼ pound sliced Cheddar cheese

¼ pound sliced pepperoni

1 large tomato, sliced

1   In a small bowl, stir together the mayonnaise, horseradish, lemon juice, salt, and pepper.

2   Split the French loaf in half and spread both cut sides of the loaf with the horseradish mayonnaise. Spread the lettuce evenly over the bottom loaf and layer the toppings, starting with the turkey, then Swiss cheese, ham, Cheddar cheese, pepperoni and tomato slices. Top with the top half of the loaf, mayonnaise side down and cut into 4 equal pieces. Serve immediately.

 Heroes don't need to eat their darn veggies—if you can't get tomatoes and lettuce, leave 'em out.

COLD
FORAGE

There hadn't been much to hunt in the woods, and now Daryl was too close to town to find anything worth shooting at all. Good thing he knew poison oak from parsley.

He came across a gazebo swallowed by honeysuckle, surrounded by a weedy garden. He sat down on a bench to rest and think about dinner. He had some pitas and a little jar of yogurt the yoga ladies had pushed on him. Probiotic this and whole-grain that. His gut squirmed just thinking about all that hippie stuff. But he didn't have much of a choice.

He dug through the garden. Pockets of mint and cress were holding out bravely against the ravenous weeds. He picked what he needed, then pulled the thorny weeds around the edible plants. They had a right to survive, too.

The weeds hid more than herbs, though. He found a detached forearm, its skin dried tight, still wearing a medical ID bracelet. A rag of skin covered the name, but whoever it was, in addition to having a missing an arm, was allergic to penicillin.

The salad sandwich was better than no sandwich at all. And anyway, he didn't really feel like eating meat anymore.

IN-THE-WEEDS STUFFED PITA WITH GARLIC YOGURT DRESSING

serves 3

1 garlic clove, peeled

3 tablespoons plain Greek yogurt

1 teaspoon white wine vinegar

¼ teaspoon salt, plus more as needed

½ teaspoon freshly ground black pepper

¼ cup olive oil

1 small bunch watercress (about 3 cups)

½ small cucumber, peeled and thinly sliced

1 tablespoon minced fresh mint

2 tablespoons minced fresh basil

3 pita breads, halved

1   Violently smash the garlic clove with a pinch of salt and crush into
     a smooth paste. In a small bowl, combine the garlic paste, yogurt,
     vinegar, salt, and pepper. Stir in the olive oil. Set aside.

2   In a medium bowl, toss together the watercress, cucumber, mint,
     and basil. Dress with garlic yogurt until just coated. Open up the pita
     halves and stuff the salad into the pockets. Serve.

PRO TIP Knowing what herbs, greens, and other vegetables grow
wild in your area can mean the difference between
snacking like a king and dying like a rat.

BANG YOUR HEAD

Daryl was at the edge of town now. The houses were closer together and the only sound in the twilight was the crickets. But more houses meant more biters.

He came to a rundown split-level that looked like some lowlife's squat. There was no decoration inside except a faded Motörhead poster. Kind of place where you just drank till you fell down, puked in the backyard, and raised hell all night long. It felt like home.

In a room with colorless carpet he found a beat-up boom box with a cassette tape still in it. He pulled out the tape—"Metal Mix." Shit, he bet he knew every song on there by heart. Batteries looked good. He was sorely tempted to flip it on just for old times' sake.

Daryl had spent a big part of his life in places like this. Had the world really changed that much? Did he miss those friends, the alcoholic assholes whose names he couldn't recall? Where had the past gone? Where was the girl who'd fed him sandwiches?

He felt a wolf clawing at his insides. No, he could never let anyone close to that beast. But that girl had tamed it a little. The girl had been timid, pretty, and generous, but strong inside. He'd never worked up the nerve to touch her, but, man, he had demolished those sandwiches.

A sound in the backyard woke him from a shallow sleep. He spied six biters back there. Probably more coming. He was too tired to fight.

It was time to party.

He lit a small fire with newspapers in the middle of the room. In the smoky light he cranked up the boom box and hit play.

The flickering light and thundering bass drew the walkers into the house. Safely outside the window he could see them swaying mindlessly around the smoky room, looking around for something to eat, the thudding metal shaking the windows.

It looked pretty much exactly like his life before the outbreak.

He left it behind him without regrets. But he slammed his head to the music as he walked toward his goal in the light of the rising sun.

UP ALL NIGHT BREAKFAST SANDWICH

makes 4 sandwiches

½ cup mayonnaise

1½ tablespoons hot sauce

1 tablespoon fresh lemon juice

Coarse kosher salt

Freshly ground black pepper

1 large russet potato, peeled

4 slices bacon, cut in half lengthwise

2 tablespoons butter

4 large eggs

4 large English muffins, split and lightly toasted

1 cup grated Cheddar cheese

2 cups arugula or lettuce

1 In a small bowl, whisk together the mayonnaise, hot sauce, and lemon juice. Season with salt and pepper.

2 Line a medium bowl with a clean dishtowel. Grate the potato directly into the towel-lined bowl. Gather the dishtowel in a bundle and squeeze in a death grip until the potato is dry.

3 Place a large skillet over medium-high heat. Add the bacon and cook until browned and crisp. Transfer to a paper towel–lined plate.

4 Spoon half of the bacon fat into a bowl and return the skillet to the heat. Add half of the potatoes and toss with the bacon fat. Using a spatula, divide the potatoes into four 3-inch round, flat cakes. Cook, turning once, until the hash browns are golden brown and crisp, 8 to 10 minutes. Transfer the rounds to a baking sheet, season with salt, and repeat.

5 Wipe out the skillet with a paper towel and add a tablespoon of butter. Return to medium heat and swirl the pan until the butter melts. Add 2 eggs and fry to taste. Season with salt and pepper. Transfer the eggs to a plate and repeat.

6 Place the English muffin halves, toasted sides up, on a plate. Spread each with a tablespoon of the spicy mayonnaise and top with a hash brown round. Sprinkle ¼ cup of the Cheddar on top of each bottom half. Top the cheese with 2 pieces of the bacon and carefully place an egg on top of the bacon. Top with ½ cup of the arugula and place each second muffin half on top, hash brown side down. Serve immediately.

PRO TIP

Be prepared for morning munchies. Put one of these together and take it with you as you flee for your life.

THOSE WHO ARRIVE
SURVIVE

He shot bolt after bolt into oncoming walkers. Then he pulled them out and reloaded. The supermarket parking lot was busy this morning.

He stuck his knife to the hilt through the bridge of the last dead thing's nose. It swooned and fell with an oozy squish. Finally he could shop.

The gleaming supermarket was dark and quiet. He banged the hatchet handle on the window a few times, then waited a few seconds. Nothing came. *Let's do this,* he said to himself.

He scanned the produce aisle through his crossbow scope. Among the moldy bins he found the remains of a walker in a stockboy's apron, his head lopped off and split like a pumpkin. Daryl hadn't been the first to shop here, then.

He put his head to the floor to look for what others missed. Under the shelves were a can of tuna, a package of Slim Jims, a bottle of beer, some birthday candles, a box of cake mix. There were also some very old peaches and a lot of dead bugs. That stockboy had been out of commission for a long time.

TUNA SALAD MELTDOWNS

makes 4 sandwiches

2 (6-ounce) cans tuna packed in olive oil, drained
¾ cup mayonnaise
2 celery stalks, finely chopped
2 whole scallions, thinly sliced
2 hard-cooked eggs, chopped
Juice of 1 lemon (about 2 tablespoons)
¾ teaspoon celery salt
1 teaspoon freshly ground black pepper
2 tablespoons finely chopped Italian flat-leaf parsley
4 slices multigrain or white Pullman bread
4 ounces Gruyere cheese, grated (about 1 cup)
8 tomato slices

1 In a medium bowl, combine the tuna, mayo, celery, scallions, eggs, lemon juice, celery salt, black pepper, and parsley and mix well.

2 Preheat the broiler on low and place a rack on the top shelf of the oven. Line a rimmed baking sheet with foil and lay out the slices of bread. Toast for 1 to 2 minutes on each side or until crisp and golden. Evenly distribute the tuna salad on the pieces of toast and top each with a quarter of the grated cheese. Transfer the baking sheet to the top rack and broil for 4 to 5 minutes, or until the cheese is melted and beginning to brown. Transfer to plates, top each with two tomato slices, and serve.

Canned tuna is at peak condition for 3 to 5 years. If the outbreak continues longer than that, tuna salad won't be much help.

A LAST GOLDEN HOPE

The winter after his brother had left for the Marines, Daryl's only friend had told him she was moving away from the mountains with her family. Locust Grove was far. He hadn't said a thing. He'd probably be better off on his own, anyway. He couldn't meet her eyes.

Finally she'd handed him one last lunch bag and kissed him on the cheek. He couldn't say good-bye. He'd just watched her back as she ran off.

In the bag was a grilled cheese, but not just any grilled cheese. It was pimento cheese. Exactly like his mother used to make him before she'd died. He must have told the girl. Now she was gone.

Just the thought of that last kindness was something he kept hallowed in his mind during the worst years of his life. No one had ever cared what he liked except her.

Pam. Her name had been Pam. A ray of light from a vanished world.

And that was why he'd come to this supermarket. Sure enough, he had tracked down what he'd been looking for this whole time.

A couple boxes of Velveeta.

He'd make grilled pimento cheese for them. Yeah, it was just a damn sandwich, but that was the point. It was the tiniest thing, a thing people used to do for each other before the dead rose to screw up everything. It was a taste of home, of family, of the world before it went to shit. He had to share it.

A world with grilled cheese was still a world worth fighting for.

SAVING GRACE GRILLED PIMENTO CHEESE

makes 8 sandwiches

PIMENTO CHEESE

8 ounces (2 cups) shredded sharp Cheddar cheese

8 ounces (2 cups) shredded Monterey Jack cheese

8 ounces (1 cup) cream cheese, softened

⅔ cup mayonnaise

2 scallions, white and green parts, thinly sliced

1 teaspoon fresh lemon juice, or more to taste

1 teaspoon dry mustard powder

1 (6-ounce) jar pimientos, drained and finely chopped

½ teaspoon freshly ground black pepper

Hot sauce, to taste

Splash of Worcestershire

1 jalapeño, seeded and deveined, if desired, and minced

SANDWICHES

16 slices white or whole-wheat bread

¼ cup (½ stick) unsalted butter, softened, or ¼ cup mayonnaise

1   Mix all the pimento cheese ingredients until smooth.

2   Make sandwiches using ½ cup pimento cheese mixture for each. Spread the butter or mayo on the outsides of all the sandwiches.

3   Heat a nonstick skillet over medium heat. Fry the sandwiches one at a time until the bread is golden and the cheese melted, about 2 minutes per side.

4   Halve the sandwiches and serve.

Be sure to make enough for your whole group. Scarcity of grilled cheese can cause dissention and even mutiny within survivor groups.

THREE
MESSY BITES
FOR THE NEWLY DEAD

THE LIVING ARE JUST A SPECIES OF THE DEAD

Pam! Oh my God. Pam!"

The voices of her fellow refugees sounded distant. She'd fed and fought beside these people during the year since Earl and Ronnie had turned. She felt them pull the walker off her chest, but she couldn't move her limbs. A vicious bite on her side burned like she'd been shot with a habanero.

The biter had crept up on her while she was heedlessly making toast by her tent. Rookie mistake. One she'd never have a chance to repeat. She closed her eyes.

She felt the pizza peel underneath her, still strapped to her back. She had tried to keep civilization alive with cooking. But the dead have numbers on their side, and they're so much hungrier.

"Fast, you have to kill me," she implored the man in the orange fishing vest as he crouched over her. She shut her eyes. "Please feed my babies. Take care of them like they were your own."

He glanced nervously in the direction of the two biter children, muzzled and tethered to a tree. Then his eyes grew wide. He had no time to answer.

When she looked up at him again he had fled. A gurgling pack of biters chased after him. She heard screaming in the distance. Then she was alone.

The man hadn't brained her, and she couldn't move. The trees swayed gently above her, and Earl rattled his chain.

So there *were* monsters in the woods. The chupacabra was real. She didn't blame Daryl for not saving her from it, but she wished he was still around somewhere.

She didn't miss what was gone anymore. She had kept her family together despite everything. She had fed so many others, and kept her standards as high as possible. She had done her best in difficult circumstances.

Once, she had been just some shy girl afraid of her own shadow, and Daryl had put his hand around hers on the hatchet handle. Lordy, he had been good-looking. He had promised to protect her.

Right now she'd trade him all the grilled cheese sandwiches in the world if he could just sink that old hatchet in her head.

She had a splitting headache, chills, and her neck began to stiffen. The light of the sun burned into her brain. But those sensations were gradually eclipsed by a ravenous hunger. It started from the wound and spread like a brush fire through her whole body. It wasn't just her stomach that was hungry—every cell in her began to scream with famine. As her life ebbed away, a brutal craving was coming to take its place.

She had done everything she could. Now she waited helplessly for the inevitable.

Things were about to get messy.

LEARNING
TO WALK

She staggered mindlessly through an agonized fog. Every move- ment hurt, but stillness hurt more. The world was nothing but indistinct lights, muffled sounds, and a crazy sea of smells. Noth- ing came before and nothing after. She bumped three times against the same tree.

She had wandered for what might have been hours or years, when a new smell struck her like lightning. An unbearable burning hunger spread from her nose to her gut until it engulfed her. She had to eat. Now.

She saw images of herself biting, and gnawing, and swallowing. The smell made her brain writhe with craving. She had to snack.

The maddeningly delicious odor was trying to hide from her. She choked with rage that the one thing that could take away her distress refused itself to her. It wanted her to suffer.

The snack was sealed in a wooden shack. Thumping on the walls didn't open it, so she hammered at the glass. The shards caught on her skin as she crawled through the broken opening, but she didn't mind. It was snack time.

She caught it by the thigh as it tried to escape and took a taste. It was *unbelievably* hard to chew through muscle, but she put all her force into her jaws. The snack kept trying to twist away. She threw herself down on top of it to quell its thrashing and kept eating. The screaming and writh- ing finally died away, and she gnashed and tore in peace.

She savored her meal. The long, ropy limbs weren't as good as the rich, wet middle, so she laid those aside and gnawed the juicy ribs.

This was a good snack, tasty enough, but she felt that with a little effort she could do much better. In any case, the hunger was flowing back fast. She wasn't nearly full.

Being a walker was no picnic.

MAPLE BRINED PORK CHOPS WITH RED-EYES GRAVY

serves 2

¼ cup maple syrup

¼ cup light brown sugar

3 tablespoons salt, plus more to taste

4 fresh thyme sprigs

1 teaspoon freshly ground black pepper, plus more to taste

2 (1-inch thick) bone-in pork chops

2 tablespoons olive oil

½ cup strong brewed black coffee

1 teaspoon Dijon mustard

2 tablespoons unsalted butter

1 In a large heavy-duty resealable plastic bag, combine 3 cups of water, the maple syrup, light brown sugar, salt, thyme sprigs, and black pepper. Seal and shake it up to dissolve the salt. Add the pork chops to the bag and let sit anywhere for 30 minutes at room temperature or refrigerate for up to 4 hours. If chilled, let chops come to room temperature for 30 minutes prior to cooking.

2 Heat a large skillet over high heat, then add the olive oil and let heat for 30 seconds. Using paper towels, dry the pork chops and add to the pan. Sear, undisturbed, for 3 to 4 minutes or until well browned. Flip the pork and cook for an additional 3 to 5 minutes, turning and searing the edges as needed, until a meat thermometer inserted into the pork reads 135°F. Transfer the pork to a cutting board, tent with foil, and let rest 10 minutes before carving.

3 Meanwhile, make the gravy. Over high heat, add the coffee to the pan and simmer, scraping up the brown bits, until reduced, about 3 minutes. Stir in the mustard, turn off the heat, and stir in the butter. Season with salt and pepper as needed. Serve the pork chops drizzled with the gravy.

PRO TIP

Hearty traditional dishes look most appetizing when served in a manner that conveys informality. These pork chops take on a devil-may-care look on a rustic wood surface.

FREAKS
AND GEEKS

Daryl kept to the woods and open fields. He was in a hurry to get back to the others with the supplies, but the state road was nothing but an all-you-can-eat buffet for the biters. Anyway, he still hoped to bag some quail or a wild hog.

A patch of color a ways off caught his eye. He crept through the brush. Tucked in a corner of a wide meadow were four tents surrounded by a makeshift fence, a whole bunch of cooking equipment, and the remains of a campfire.

Some of the campers were still there, at least parts of them. They lay where the biters had surprised them, still wrapped in the chewed tatters of their sleeping bags. Unsteady footprints led off south toward the road. He guessed five or six biters, probably off somewhere picking goose-down out of their teeth right now.

He picked up a jar of mustard from the supplies around the fire. The campers weren't going to miss the Grey Poupon now.

There was a bloodied depression in the grass a few feet from the fire pit. Someone had fallen and bled out, but they weren't there now. A set of meandering tracks led off in the direction he was headed. He was pretty sure he didn't want to run into whatever made them, but he better keep track of where it went. He didn't need anything coming back to bite him.

He followed the tracks toward the edge of the meadow, where he could soon make out two figures. They were just kids, or had been. A boy and a girl, chained to a tree and snapping at him like famished pit bulls.

Daryl squinted and raised his lip. Just when he thought this world couldn't get more messed up.

"Well, ain't you a sorry-looking pair," he said aloud.

The girl rolled her eyes at him and made a gurgling sound.

"Right back at ya, Sunshine."

UNSUSPECTING PIGS IN BLANKETS

serves 6

6 hot dogs

All-purpose flour, for dusting

1 sheet frozen puff pastry, thawed (about 8 ounces)

1 large egg

1 tablespoon water

2 tablespoons poppy seeds (optional)

2 tablespoons finely chopped bread and butter pickles

2 tablespoons finely chopped dill pickles

Mustard, for serving

Ketchup, for serving

1 Poke hot dogs several times with the tip of a knife.

2 On a lightly floured work surface, roll the puff pastry into a 15-by-11-inch rectangle. Cut lengthwise into three 5-inch-wide strips. Cut each strip in half crosswise so you have 6 pieces of puff.

3 In a small bowl, beat together the egg and water. Line baking sheets with parchment paper or a nonstick baking mat. Place a hot dog on the narrow end of one piece of pastry. Roll to enclose, brushing with some of the beaten egg to adhere; transfer to prepared baking sheet. Repeat the process with remaining hot dogs and pastry. Brush the tops of puff pastry with the egg wash and sprinkle with poppy seeds if using. Transfer to refrigerator and let chill for 15 minutes.

4 Preheat oven to 450°F. Bake the hot dogs until the pastry is puffed and golden, about 20 minutes.

5 In a small bowl combine the bread and butter pickles and the dill pickles. Carefully split the puff pastry along one side of each of the pigs in blankets and top with the pickle relish. Serve with mustard and ketchup.

These classic tidbits need not be boring or staid—a bright splatter of ketchup can make an eye-opening presentation.

YOU'VE GOT
RED ON YOU

Maybe there was hope for the living, but it sure as hell wasn't inside this shack.

The tracks had led him more or less west, toward home. If this particular biter was headed for his friends, he had to stop it.

Its reckless spoor was typical enough. Besides the lumbering footprints and the mangled undergrowth, rags of flesh still clung to the trees where the dead thing had passed.

He found an old shovel, like what they use for pizzas. He'd be sure to keep an eye out for a biter with mustachios, an apron, and a big chef hat. Next to the shovel lay an unlucky woodchuck, picked cleaner than he could have done himself, let alone a sloppy biter.

Daryl had always wolfed down his food, like he thought it was going to run off. Pam used to laugh and tell him to slow down. Let yourself taste it, she'd say. He never knew how to repay those embarrassing kindnesses. She had really wanted to know how to butcher her own food. He'd never met a girl who liked hunting and killing so much.

He'd wrapped his trembling hand over Pam's on the hatchet handle. *First you chop the head . . .*

When he found the shack even the birds were quiet. The door was locked and the window was busted inward. So far, a pretty typical walker kill zone. But inside was another story.

"Fussy carnage," was the only way he could think of to describe the scene. Usually biters left a bloody mess splattered around the place like spin-art.

This biter had picked some parts clean and left others. What it didn't eat was stacked neatly in the corner. It clearly didn't care for elbows or knees. Even the blood looked like it had been sopped.

Biters getting picky—this was not a good sign. They were evolving.

ELBOWS CASSEROLE

serves 6 to 8

2 tablespoons olive oil, plus more for pan

1 onion, finely chopped

1 pound ground beef

Coarse kosher salt

Freshly ground black pepper

1 (28-ounce) can diced tomatoes, drained

2 cups water

1½ cups whole milk

1 tablespoon Worcestershire

1 teaspoon granulated sugar

1 teaspoon paprika

½ teaspoon cumin

2 cups (½ pound) elbow noodles

2 cups grated Cheddar cheese

½ cup Parmesan cheese

2 tablespoons finely chopped Italian flat-leaf parsley

1   Preheat the oven to 425°F. Heat a large skillet set over medium-high heat, then add the oil. Add the chopped onion and cook, stirring occasionally, for 5 minutes. Add the ground beef and season with salt and pepper. Cook, stirring, until the beef is browned and cooked through, about 8 minutes.

2   Drain off the excess fat and add the tomatoes, water, milk, Worcestershire, sugar, paprika, and cumin and stir to combine. Add the pasta, cover the pan, and bring to a boil. Simmer until the pasta is almost tender, about 7 minutes. Stir in the Cheddar cheese and season with salt and pepper.

3   Pour the mixture into an oiled, shallow casserole dish and sprinkle with Parmesan cheese. Bake until the pasta is cooked through and the cheese melts, about 15 minutes. Sprinkle with parsley and serve.

PRO TIP

Great for leftovers the following night, assuming you're feeling optimistic about the future.

THERE'S NO "I" IN
SWARM

Nothing could quench the fire of craving in her gut, nor the dull, ceaseless fury it ignited. She couldn't do this alone.

Other bodies shambled nearby, but they didn't smell good. Living snacks had the sharp, sour aroma of fear. But these bodies moved slowly and smelled of nothing but shadows and hunger—just like her.

Her hunger never rested and neither did she. She followed the retreating scent of food until it grew stronger again. Soon, many famished bodies were following the same scent.

Her black hunger merged with theirs until she was just part of a blundering, ruinous swarm of biting mouths. The swarm needed snacks. She made a slurping sigh of resignation: she'd have to share.

At last the good smell was close. The inexhaustible pain she felt was the snacks' fault, for not being in her belly. She wanted to scream, but made only a choked rasp with her hardening throat.

The swarm surrounded the snacks. Lots of snacks, pointing sticks and making loud sounds. She dove at the noisy buffet, jostled by her fellow diners. A few of them fell and seemed to lose their appetite forever. Most just fed and fed.

She caught flesh in her teeth. It kept wrenching itself out of her mouth, but she pulled it back to her with delight. Other mouths came for her snack too. She tried to make sure she got the delicious bits. She could tell the others didn't really give a damn.

The swarm fed and moved on. She moved with it automatically, but her heart wasn't in it. Something in her body, like a memory embedded in her muscles, wasn't satisfied just to feed fast and dash off.

Meat was good. It just needed—something.

MUSTARD-RUBBED LONG PORK

serves 4

2 tablespoons olive oil
1 pork tenderloin (about 1 pound)
Coarse kosher salt
Freshly ground black pepper
2 tablespoons Dijon mustard
1 tablespoon whole-grain mustard
1 tablespoon brown sugar

1 Preheat the oven to 400°F. Heat a large, ovenproof skillet over medium-high heat, then add the oil. Season the pork tenderloin with salt and pepper. Add the pork to the hot oil and sear until golden brown on all sides, 8 to 10 minutes.

2 In a medium bowl, whisk together the Dijon and whole-grain mustards and the brown sugar.

3 Transfer the pork to the oven and roast for 5 minutes. Brush the meat generously with half of the mustard mixture and return to the oven to roast until an instant-read thermometer inserted into the thickest part of the pork registers 140°F, 7 to 10 minutes. Transfer to a plate, cover with foil, and let rest for at least 10 minutes.

4 Pour the reserved mustard sauce into a small saucepan and heat over medium until just warmed through. Slice the tenderloin and serve with the warm mustard sauce.

PRO TIP   Ingredient substitutions are unavoidable when the world has ended. However, there is no morally defensible substitution for pork.

OM NOM NOM NOM

The walker left a trail of weird crumbs.

He found several more carefully arranged feed areas and a quail with one nibble taken from it as if it had been rejected. He picked up a gore-smeared cleaver that looked like it'd been through ten flavors of hell.

The walker had veered off north. It was no longer on his way home, but he couldn't let it go now. Something about the way this thing ate wasn't biter-like. It fed almost like a person. Well, if that person was Hannibal Lecter.

He crossed an empty field and passed a cairn of rocks. On the other side of it sat a lone walker in pajamas.

It reached for him with hands that were nothing but skeleton. It couldn't even grab him—the finger bones just flopped around on slack tendons like a rubber toy. It gurgled at him in frustration.

He stuck his knife though its rubbery forehead. "Go back to sleep," he said, curling his lip.

He looked closely at the carcass. The walker's flesh was still moist. It hadn't turned more than a day before. There wasn't much sign of what turned it either, except for the fleshless hands and forearms. It was as if it had been nibbled—carefully.

A walker didn't eat itself. Something had done this to him. Something that particularly liked finger meat. Something with peculiar tastes. There was an almost dainty quality about it. He recognized the handiwork of his walker. The thing could have written a cookbook: *To Serve Man*. He laughed at his own joke.

He caught himself thinking about Pam again. She had once told him how she liked to take the chicken feet from her grandma's stew pot and suck them clean. He'd told her she was probably a sicko. She had just laughed and kept on kicking her feet slowly in the creek water.

Nothing disgusted Daryl more than walkers. But deep inside he had to admit he admired this one's discrimination. This was not your average biter.

NAIL-BITER CHICKEN FINGERS

serves 6 to 8

1 pound chicken breasts, patted dry

Coarse kosher salt

Freshly ground black pepper

½ cup all-purpose flour

2 large eggs, beaten

1 cup panko (Japanese bread crumbs)

1 cup crushed potato chips

4 tablespoons peanut or vegetable oil, or more
as needed

½ cup ketchup

½ teaspoon Sriracha or other hot sauce,
plus more to taste

1 Cut the chicken breasts into 2-inch long strips, each ½ inch wide.
   Lay the chicken pieces out on a baking sheet and season liberally
   with salt and pepper. Refrigerate, uncovered, for 30 minutes.

2 Put the flour in one medium bowl and the eggs in another medium
   bowl. In a third medium bowl, combine the panko and the crushed
   potato chips; season with pepper and stir to combine.

3 Dip each chicken strip in the flour, shaking off any excess, then dip
   into the eggs, and then into the potato chip mixture, turning to coat
   completely. Transfer to a clean baking sheet.

4 Place a large skillet over medium-high heat and add 2 tablespoons
   of oil. Once the oil is shimmering, add enough of the chicken strips
   to fit comfortably in one layer. Sear, without moving, until the chicken
   fingers are golden brown on one side, 4 to 5 minutes. Flip over the
   chicken fingers and cook until the chicken is golden brown on the
   second side, 4 to 5 minutes. Transfer the chicken to a paper towel–
   lined plate and add 2 tablespoons oil to the skillet. Once the oil is
   hot, repeat with more chicken strips, adding more oil to the pan if
   you need to fry a third batch.

5 In a medium bowl, stir together the ketchup and Sriracha. Serve the
   chicken fingers warm with the Sriracha ketchup.

PRO TIP

Know your
survivor group:
are they
ravenous or
peckish? These
tasty tidbits
can be an hors
d'oeuvre or a
whole meal.

PROTECTION

The picky walker moved in looping circles, like it was in a giant supermarket without a list.

Daryl found a freshly killed sheep, its belly chewed open. A coyote would have eaten through the rear. This was either the work of a biter or a chupacabra. But a chupacabra wouldn't have left the pretty little pile of herbs next to its meal. He figured he was still on the trail.

The terrain got drier and he began to lose its tracks. He lay down to side-head a grassy stretch and saw a shiny spot where the biter had tripped or fallen. There were depressions in the leaves here and there, showing it had come through recently. But finally he lost the trail altogether, and even by circling he couldn't pick it back up.

The light was failing and he had to find somewhere to spend the night. Last thing he needed was a swarm of biters tripping over him in the night.

He found an old sawmill, filled up with dead machines slowly rusting to powder. Enormous wheels with red teeth the size of his head bit halfway into unfinished planks. The honeysuckle was starting to strangle this place like everywhere else in these parts.

As night stretched on, he pulled his poncho around himself and tried to sleep. In his dream he saw the girl, grabbing hold of the hatchet for the first time. *First you chop the head,* he was saying. . . .

A sound woke him, something on the shop floor. He grabbed his hatchet with both hands and crouched in the darkness, flashlight clamped between his teeth.

CAT HEAD BISCUITS WITH SAWMILL GRAVY

serves 6

BISCUITS

3 cups self-rising flour, plus additional for dusting

1½ cups buttermilk

2 tablespoons unsalted butter, softened and cut into pieces

GRAVY

1 pound breakfast sausage, casings removed (or use bulk sausage meat)

¼ cup all-purpose flour

2¼ cups milk

¼ teaspoon salt, or more to taste

½ teaspoon freshly ground black pepper

1 Preheat the oven to 400°F. Line a baking sheet with parchment paper or lightly grease it.

2 In a bowl, gently stir together the flour, buttermilk, and butter until the dough just comes together. On a floured surface, pat the dough into a 1½-inch-thick round. Cut the dough into 6 rounds that are 4 inches in diameter and transfer to the baking sheet. Bake until golden brown, 20 to 25 minutes.

3 To make the gravy, crumble the sausage into a heated skillet and cook until brown all over, about 5 minutes; drain the meat on a paper towel–lined plate. Leave the fat in the pan.

4 Return the skillet to the stove over medium heat. Whisk in the flour and cook for 2 minutes. Slowly whisk in the milk; increase the heat to medium high and simmer, whisking constantly, until thickened, about 3 minutes.

5 Stir in the sausage and season the gravy with salt and pepper. To serve, split the biscuits and top with generous spoonfuls of gravy.

PRO TIP

So-called because they're about the size of a cat's skull, cat head biscuits make a hearty breakfast any time of day. Just try not to think too hard about skulls.

CHUPACABRA

She hunted alone again, far from the swarm. She didn't mind sharing, but the swarm had no standards. Alone, she could be choosy. She didn't have to just take whatever she could grab.

Snacks were near. Not the kind of snack that ran around screaming, but small snacks in wooly wrappers that stuck in her teeth. They might fill her until a really fulfilling nosh came her way.

She tackled one as it slept and took a big bite.

"Baaaa!" said the snack.

But it wasn't really up to snuff. Something wasn't right. She paused and stared blankly at her dinner. Hunger burned her from the inside out, but her hands wouldn't bring the snack to her mouth. Her frustration grew.

She shambled over to some tall grass. She ripped some fragrant leafy plants up by the roots and returned to her meal with them. She dropped them tentatively on the mound of carnage. The plant wouldn't help fill her hunger, but the smell was nice and it enhanced the overall experience. She went back to chewing.

When she was done she stumbled around after the other wooly snacks for a long time, but they were awake now and trotted away faster than she could follow.

Somehow she knew this was all wrong. Nothing satisfied her. The dark painful hunger drove her ever onward, but she knew she could do better with a little effort. She just wanted the pain and hunger to end.

Eventually she wandered out of the trees and saw a building with a door. She had her heart set on the shrieking, fearful snacks that she loved best, and buildings with doors were where they usually were.

The awful hunger had already caught up with her again. It drove her inside.

CHUPACABRA SHEPHERD'S PIE

serves 6

2 pounds russet potatoes, peeled and cut into 1-inch chunks

1 tablespoon plus 1 teaspoon salt, plus more as needed

½ cup heavy cream or whole milk, or more as needed

4 tablespoons unsalted butter

1 tablespoon olive oil

1 small onion, chopped

1 large carrot, peeled and chopped

1 pound lean ground beef

½ pound ground lamb

1 teaspoon dried thyme

½ teaspoon freshly ground black pepper

2 tablespoons Worcestershire sauce

1 tablespoon tomato paste

½ cup dry white wine

½ cup fresh or frozen peas

¼ cup chopped fresh Italian flat-leaf parsley, plus more for serving

1 Fill a medium pot with cold water, add the potatoes and 1 teaspoon salt. Bring to a boil over high heat and then cook until potatoes are fork tender, about 15 minutes. Drain the potatoes and return them to the pot.

2 In a small pot over low heat, warm the cream and melt the butter. Add the warm mixture to the cooked potatoes and, with a masher or fork, mash the potatoes. If the potatoes are too dry, add more cream or milk as needed. Add 1 teaspoon of salt, or to taste, and set aside.

3 Preheat the oven to 425°F. Heat the olive oil in a large skillet over high heat. Add the onion and carrot and sauté until tender, about 5 minutes. Add the beef and lamb, using your spoon to break up the meat. Stirring occasionally, cook until browned and cooked through, about 10 minutes. Drain any excess fat and then add the dried thyme, 2 teaspoons salt, black pepper, Worcestershire, tomato paste, and white wine. Stir to combine and cook until the wine is reduced, about 7 minutes. Turn off the heat and then fold in the peas and parsley.

4 Place a 1½- to 2-quart baking dish on a rimmed baking sheet. Spread the meat mixture over the bottom of the baking dish and then spread the mashed potatoes over the surface. Bake for 20 to 25 minutes, or until the surface of the potatoes is golden brown. Let cool for 15 minutes and then serve garnished with more chopped parsley.

PRO TIP

A garnish provides a striking contrast to the eye as well as the taste buds, supplying a boost to morale in a world ruled by wilted undead.

I COULD JUST
EAT YOU UP

Something smelled really, really good. Something that was more than a snack, something that made her whole body wobble.

The building was dark and twisty. Large sharp things sat everywhere. But she was sure if she looked hard enough, she'd find the snack.

As the scent grew more distinct, even her raging hunger couldn't mask a new feeling that was working its way upward inside her. Images ran through her decomposing brain. Someone's hand on hers. Hunting together. Sleepy sexy eyes. Taking the head off a snack, not with her teeth, but with a sharp, metal gleam. She liked the gleam. She dreaded it, but it comforted her.

She followed the luscious scent with halting steps. The snack stood there waiting for her. The snack didn't run. Good snack, good. End this hunger. Nothing else mattered.

The snack stood up from behind a large machine. It had big, juicy arms that made her feel itchy. This was the snack for her, had always been the one for her.

She felt her body leaning forward, mouth first. She wanted to feed on it. She wanted to feed it. She wanted just to look at it. She opened her arms. Did it want her as much as she wanted it?

The snack raised an arm and moved forward, a bright, cutting gleam in its hand. The sharp thing whistled sweetly and plunged deep into her head. The last vestige of her rotted brain stem surged and went dark.

She went limp and fell with a grateful gurgle. The hunger had left her in peace at last.

SWEET-ISH FLESHBALLS WITH RED BERRIES
makes about 36 meatballs

3 tablespoons unsalted butter

1 garlic clove, finely chopped

½ onion, finely chopped

1 pound ground pork

½ cup bread crumbs

½ cup heavy cream

1 large egg

¼ teaspoon ground allspice

Coarse kosher salt

Freshly ground black pepper

2 tablespoons all-purpose flour

1 cup beef or chicken stock, warm

2 tablespoons sour cream

3 tablespoons finely chopped fresh parsley

¼ cup lingonberry preserves (or red currant or sour cherry preserves)

1   Preheat the oven to 425°F.

2   In a medium skillet set over medium heat melt 1 tablespoon of the butter. Add the garlic and onion and sauté until softened, about 8 minutes. Transfer the onion mixture to a large bowl. Mix in the pork, bread crumbs, ¼ cup cream, egg, and allspice. Season with salt and pepper. Use lightly dampened hands to roll the meat mixture into 1 tablespoon balls and transfer to a rimmed baking sheet. Bake until the meatballs are golden brown and cooked through, 12 to 15 minutes.

3   In a large saucepan set over medium heat melt 2 tablespoons of the butter. Whisk in the flour until a smooth paste forms. Gradually whisk in the remaining ¼ cup cream and the stock. Bring the mixture to a boil, then reduce the heat and simmer until the sauce thickens slightly, 3 to 5 minutes. Season with salt and pepper and whisk in the sour cream. Add the meatballs to the sauce and stir to coat. Divide among serving plates, sprinkle with parsley, and serve with lingonberry preserves.

Make an impact with color by drizzling the livid jam over the meat in splattered lines.

YOU GRILL OR
YOU DIE

He felt strangely sad, looking down at the biter who'd come this close to gobbling him up in his sleep.

Was this the strange creature he'd been tracking? It pretty much fit the bill, with that silkscreened skull on its sweatshirt. He tried to imagine its face before the skin had dried away, before its hair matted, and before its mouth grew stained with blood and gore. It must have had a name and a family.

He'd keep the cleaver he had found. He figured if the walker had carried it this long it must have been important. It was near as good as his hatchet. He could sharpen it up and use it.

He wondered again about Pam and her peculiar tastes. He hoped she had been spared all of this.

He gathered his stuff to set off. He wasn't far from the friends who had yelled at him, threatened his life, shot at him, and become his family since the outbreak. It had taken the snacking dead to bring kindness into his life again.

Something rustled in the brush behind the sawmill. He found hoof tracks in the mud. Could've been deer, except for the fresh rooting hole in the mud. A feral hog had just been here looking for a snack.

He was done hunting the dead. He was going to hunt himself a hog and barbecue it. He could feel the sauce running down his chin just thinking about those ribs.

But he'd wait till he got back to the group. In a world where we're all on the menu, you grill together or die alone.

The apocalypse was no picnic, but you didn't have to starve either.

DRIPPING RIBS WITH BOURBON

serves 6

RIBS

2 racks baby back ribs (5 to 6 pounds)

Kosher salt and freshly ground black pepper

1 Spanish onion, thinly sliced

1 cup pomegranate juice or orange juice

2 tablespoons cider vinegar

BARBECUE SAUCE

2 tablespoons olive oil

1 small red onion, chopped (about 1 cup)

2 garlic cloves, minced

1 tablespoon chili powder

¼ teaspoon grated orange zest

1½ cups ketchup

⅓ cup cider vinegar

¼ cup honey

¼ cup bourbon

¼ cup Dijon mustard

2 tablespoons Worcestershire sauce

1 tablespoon hot sauce, or more to taste

The meat on baby back ribs shrinks away from the bone during cooking, creating a convenient handle for picking them up. Ribs are one snack the living and the undead can all agree on.

1 Preheat the oven to 325°F. Season the ribs with salt and pepper. Scatter onions on the bottom of a large roasting pan. Place the ribs on top of the onions and pour the juice and 2 tablespoons vinegar over the top. Cover the pan tightly with foil. Bake until the ribs are very tender, about 2 hours. Store the ribs in the cooking liquid until ready to serve. Ribs can be cooked 2 days ahead.

2 To prepare the barbecue sauce, heat the oil in a large saucepan over high heat, and sauté the onion until very tender, about 10 minutes. Add the garlic and sauté for 3 minutes longer. Add the chili powder and orange zest and cook for 1 minute. Add the ketchup, vinegar, honey, bourbon, mustard, Worcestershire, and hot sauce and simmer uncovered on low heat for 15 to 20 minutes, until darker in color and very thick. Let cool then puree in a blender until smooth. Sauce can be made up to 1 week ahead.

3 Light a grill or preheat your broiler. Generously brush the ribs with the barbecue sauce and grill, basting with more sauce, until the meat is glazed all over and crisp around the edges, about 10 minutes. Serve with extra barbecue sauce on the side.

LAST CALL

After the end of the civilized world, a very bad day at work, or binge-watching a favorite TV series, a cocktail can be the one thing that stands between you and a murderous rampage. Straight spirits, wine, or beer are effective, but nothing says "society endures" quite like a mixed drink.

Make 'em strong, make 'em count.

BLOODY WALKER

Really just a Zombie by another name. The guy who invented that cocktail was a Prohibition-era bootlegger called Donn the Beachcomber, so you know it's apocalypse-ready.

serves 1

2 ounces añejo rum

1 ounce light rum

1 ounce dark rum

½ ounce lime juice

¼ ounce pomegranate juice

¼ ounce apricot brandy

¼ ounce 151-proof rum

1 or 2 dashes Angostura bitters

1 cherry, for garnish

1 pineapple spear, for garnish

1 mint sprig, for garnish

Combine all the liquid ingredients in a cocktail shaker filled with ice and shake. (Or, combine in a blender and blend on low speed, then add ½ cup of ice cubes and blend for 5 seconds on high.) Strain into a Tiki mug, Collins glass, or washed pickle jar. Add garnishes and serve with a swizzle. If no appropriate swizzle can be found, see below.

HOW TO ROAST A BONE SWIZZLE: If plastic swizzles are scant, you may be forced to resort to nature. The bone swizzle looks great and shows that you're not messing around.

Reserve a set of long, small bones from a roasted chicken: thighs, wing bones, or even drumsticks are great. Make sure all the meat and soft material has been gnawed away. Roast at 275°F for 1 to 2 hours, until thoroughly dried out. When finished, your bone swizzle will make an assertive statement in any mixed drink.

CORPSE REVIVER NO. 2

Classic hair of the biter that bit ya. As the original Savoy recipe notes, "four of these will unrevive the corpse again." An effective weapon against the boozier undead.

serves 1

¾ ounce gin
¾ ounce Cointreau
¾ ounce Lillet Blanc
¾ ounce lemon juice
Absinthe or Pernod

In a cocktail shaker filled with ice, shake the gin, Cointreu, Lillet Blanc, and lemon juice, and strain into a cocktail glass rinsed with a few drops of absinthe or Pernod. Now you're ready to face the end of the world again.

LIL' ASS-KICKER PUNCH

This is a southern concoction that kind of sneaks up before it whoops you. Strong and sweet. Not too sweet, though, Sunshine. (Adapted from *Punch* by David Wondrich.)

makes 26 cups

1½ quarts sweet tea (DIY, or any store-looted brand such as Snapple—but not a fruit-flavored variety)
1½ quarts lightly sweetened lemonade (such as Newman's Own, if you're looting)
1½ liters seltzer
1 liter Jim Beam or Jack Daniels—anything strong and southern
¾ liter Myer's white rum
3 lemons, sliced (optional)
Grated nutmeg (optional)

Stir together all the liquid ingredients in a bucket filled with ice. Garnish with sliced lemons and grated nutmeg, if you can find 'em. Guaranteed to create a swarm—in a good way.

ACKNOWLEDGMENTS

Undying thanks to all the people who helped bring this book to life.

A big zombie hug to the well-seasoned team at Clarkson Potter: Doris Cooper, Erica Gelbard, Shira Gluck, Carly Gorga, Derek Gullino, Stephanie Huntwork, Maha Khalil, Pam Krauss, Jim Massey, Mark McCauslin, Neil Spitkovsky, Jane Treuhaft, and Kate Tyler.

Heartfelt gratitude to the scrappy band of survivors responsible for the photos—splatter photographer Evan Sung, iron-toothed photo assistant Eric Bissell, food and gore stylists Suzanne Lenzer and Ashley Schleeper, and props stylist/armorer Maeve Sheridan.

Thanks to Luke Guldan for backwoods biceps, and Lily Starbuck for wielding a mean peel. Ice cream truck courtesy of Andrew Bozzo of Carpe Donut NYC. Room and board by the immortal Joe Broker.

Thanks to recipe developers Rebekah Peppler and Julia Heffelfinger for ensuring the snacks truly were to die for.

Thanks to heroic agent Janis Donnaud.

My family survived this long zombie apocalypse with patience and grace. In this world, you can't do nothin' without your flesh and blood.

INDEX